Searching Below the Surface

A Deeper Look at Covenant and Contract

Nakhati Jon

Nakhati Media

© 2022 by Nakhati Jon
All rights reserved.
ISBN: 979-8-9857602-0-0

Kindle Direct Publishing

Unless otherwise indicated, all Scripture quotations are taken from the English Standard Version, found on www.biblegateway.com Copyright © 2001 by Crossway Bibles, a publishing ministry of Good News Publishers.

Cover design by Ariel – (arielthemermaid20@gmail.com) The artist depicted the Isfahan Armenian Vank Church in Iran on the left and the Medina Mosque in Saudi Arabia on the right.

For further comments and inquiries, please see X @NakhatiJ or the author's blog https://nakhatijon.com/

Dedication

*Praise be to God who revealed Himself
to us by His Oneness
as Father, Son, and Holy Spirit.*

*Praise be to the only God, our Savior who,
through Jesus Christ our Lord grants us
the Truth, the Way and the Life.
To him be glory,
majesty, dominion, and authority,
before all time and now and forever.
Amen*

Foreword

The author, Nakhati Jon, has served for 29 years in Muslim countries, both Sunni and Shiite. It has been my privilege to know him for 38 years. He is both a practical evangelist/church planter and an excellent research scholar.

Christ made it clear that houses built on a rock foundation survive storms much better than those built on sand. This study peels back the foundations of covenant vs. contractual relationships leading to the relationship in marriage. Nakhati Jon studies the differences of contract and covenant related to their understanding of God, scripture, man's relationship with God, salvation, sanctification and an introduction for marriage. Drilling down to one's presuppositions helps to better understand one's theology and practices.

Islam is a religion of mathematics. Surah 97:3 tells us that prayer on the night of power, (Lailet al Qadr, when the Qur'an began to be delivered) is better than prayers over a thousand months, or 83 and 1/3 years. Mosques are normally packed that week. Prayer before and after the five daily prayer times provide "extra credit" from Allah. One of my students was interviewing a Saudi lady who said when she lies down to sleep, she adds up her good deeds and bad deeds to see if the good outweighed the bad deeds. At least eight times in the Qur'an, scales for measuring good and bad works are mentioned. This mathematical legalistic view of salvation and life is foundational to a contractual relationship as opposed to a covenantal relationship, based on grace.

The difference between a covenant marriage and a contractual marriage is significant. I have been told by a Muslim male that "when I get married, I am responsible to provide financially for my wife and family, and my wife is responsible to provide sex when I want it."

There is a Muslim hadith which says that if a wife dies before her husband, he is not responsible to pay for her funeral, even if he can afford it, because the contract is broken and she is not fulfilling her responsibility. (These views are not held by all Muslims.)

Nakhati Jon skillfully searches below the surface to understand the roots of the thinking of our Muslim friends and neighbors and of Christians.

Patrick Cate, Ph.D. from Hartford Seminary

Preface

Searching Below the Surface:

A Deeper Look at Covenant and Contract

Often, I walk down a central street near where I live, unaware of what lies below. Sprinkled among these modern buildings of no more than fifty years old are fountains, squares, and historic bazaars, some of which may be hundreds of years old — the ordinary streets packed with multiple forms of transportation.

I needed to visit a government office in an older area one day, but the street was down to one lane. City workers, enlarging the drainage system to help prevent flash floods, had dug a massive trench in the middle of the road. I stared in awe as the opened track revealed ancient walls, water channels, and building foundations. The work crews worked around these substructures to install a new system, even adjusting to allow the ancient elements to remain. Previously, I had walked multiple times up and down that street, entirely unaware of what lay below. The foundation of the ancient city rested just below my feet. Previously, I walked on the surface without knowing the structures beneath, but now my observation of the exposed sub-layer gave me a new perspective.

This book exposes the underlying ideas beneath our spiritual and religious systems. Below Christian and Islamic religious structures and paths hide ancient networks that need raising to the surface so that a better understanding of worldviews can occur. This book will examine how the Bible portrays a covenant viewpoint and the Quran a contract one.

How do differing creation accounts in the Bible and Quran uphold theological understandings? In what ways do the oneness of Yahweh and the Absolute Oneness of Allah influence their narratives? Each explored area hints further meaning to the whole story. What we hear about Yahweh or Allah today may not give a complete picture of what hides beneath a religious structure or mode of thinking. As in any ancient dig, time and patience provide a fuller description.

4

Likewise, the many artifacts discovered without a systematic blueprint may conceal a fuller understanding. This writing will unearth either a systematic covenant or contract blueprint. As we search and meticulously expose the substructure, a more complete picture will form to show the difference between a covenant God called Yahweh and a deity prone to contract, called Allah. *Searching Below the Surface* digs up the bedrock of why the Bible presents a covenant model and Islam a contract one. The underpinnings in each perspective reflect the essence of either Yahweh or Allah's nature to guide our exploration.

As we journey intellectually into the Bible and Quran, we will appreciate how Christianity and Islam pursue divergent paths concerning life. We will see a different viewpoint based on the nature of deity's oneness, what God says about man, and how he interacts and offers deliverance for humanity. These things influence a follower's identity and relationships. Any archeologist takes much time collecting and classifying the artifacts discovered to categorize the evidence. Theological archeology examines how the Bible and Quran each formulate a collective identity. The items gathered from both sides, with much patient analysis, will create classifications for study.

The biblical source extensively draws, defines, and legitimizes a covenant identity. On the other hand, the Islamic source often ignores the biblical context to rearrange, re-define and re-legitimize a contract parameter regarding marriage. These textual digs will explore the distinctions and inferences that eventually show marriage as covenantal or contractual. As in any archaeological dig, the study of the area requires much patient evaluation. An archeologist finds obvious and common objects but provides a fuller picture when comparing the finds with other objects and time periods. Likewise, we discover a covenant or contract identity when contrasting the Bible and the Quran. We hope to show that Yahweh, a covenant God, and Allah, a contract one, eventually affect people's views of marriage.

A few notes of clarification

1) Yahweh is the Hebrew name (יְהֹוָה – YHWH) for God, used in the Old Testament, and Allah (الله) is the Arabic name for God, used in the Quran. For the sake of clarity, *Searching Below the Surface* will use the Old Testament name for God to describe the God of the Bible and Allah (الله) to depict the god of the Quran.

2) A surah refers to a chapter in the Quran.

3) Islamic references will come from the Sunni perspective, with Shia references stated as such. 4) this writing will omit the Islamic tradition of preceding or following prophets' names with a phrase of honor for brevity's sake.

5) "The Bible" and "The Quran" will refer to various English translations of each.

6) When referring to deity, "he" will not be capitalized mid-sentence, except in quotations.

7) Many new terms exist in this writing. When needed, the Appendix displays a *Definition of Terms*.

Searching Below the Surface is the foundational book to the series *Exploring Marriage in an Islamic Context*. The book will study and contrast covenant and contractual designs from both perspectives. This writing searches foundational issues and sometimes will peruse core ideas that influence a marriage definition. The depth and practicality concerning marriage will come in the books to follow. This book will open the door to the next book, defining marriage and how couples should live out that definition. Later books will show how to teach the marriage passages of Genesis and Ephesians in an Islamic setting.

You are invited as a husband, wife, engaged couple, inquiring student, or inquisitive teacher to explore these vastly different foundations. *Searching Below the Surface* invites you to search for an identity that results from these beliefs, leading us to discover why the biblical narrative promotes covenantal ideas, not contractual ones. May the uncovered foundations grant you a better appreciation for God's great covenantal love for each of us!

Chapter 1 – Partakers or Spectators of God's Oneness?

"The secret things belong to the LORD our God, but the things that are revealed belong to us and to our children forever, that we may do all the words of this law." Deuteronomy 29:29, [1]

God *"has granted to us his precious and very great promises, so that through them you may become partakers of the divine nature."* 2 Peter 1:4

"Only God knows God." Al-Junayd

On another scorching, sweltering day in Central Asia, we traveled in our rented taxi to the capital. Per custom, my wife sat in the back with our kids while I sat in the front, chatting with the driver. Dust and welcome air flew in through the open windows, and we talked loudly to drown out the wind. Then, the inevitable conversation began:

Driver: Central Asian women are beautiful, aren't they? (My back prickled in response to my wife's almost-palpable eye-roll.)

Me: My wife is beautiful.

Driver: You should get a second wife. (I felt my wife rethinking pacifism.)

Me: (Emphatically) God is one! Therefore, I will have only one wife!

Driver: Oh—this is true! (Pause) Does your wife speak the language?

Me: Fluently. And she doesn't like what you're saying.

Years later, my wife confessed she had ignored the illogic of the "One God/one wife" statement in return for its success as a conversation-stopper. But in researching, I happily discovered my shot at philosophy had been logical after all. In fact, my bit of accidental wisdom carried foundational truths about Yahweh's nature, his relationship with man, and his plan for marriage.

Yahweh's Oneness and Allah's Absolute Oneness

The oneness of God differs between Christianity and Islam. The God of the Bible presents himself in oneness formed within a unity of divine persons. At the same time, the Islamic view promotes the oneness of Allah as absolutely alone without any other. Oneness in Unity[2] (Trinity) marks the biblical essence of deity, while Absolute Oneness describes the Islamic viewpoint.

I like to stress God's Oneness in ministry since both Christians and Muslims readily agree on monotheism. Finding commonalities establishes a good starting point for dialogue. Yet, the elephant in the room, which every Muslim knows, is that Allah has no partner nor grants any to bear his image, and every Christian knows that the God of the Bible has a Son and bestows his image on humanity. Also, how does either side define God's oneness? Let us respectfully explore these different ideas of oneness, which will reveal how each perspective forms a different foundation.

The two questions in describing God's Oneness lie before us:

1. Is God a unity of divine persons?
2. Or is he absolutely alone?

On that note, we will start with the Islamic ideas concerning the Absolute Oneness of Allah to form a semblance of contrast. Absolute Oneness describes Allah as one who has no partners, no son, and no likeness, so he is utterly alone.

Allah's Absolute Oneness

Surah 112:1–4 summarizes Allah's oneness: *"Say: He, Allah, **is One**. [2] Allah is He on Whom all depend. [3] He begets not, nor is He begotten. [4] And **none is like Him**."* (bold mine Surah 112:1–4)[3] Depending on one's interpretation these verses on the surface could be true of Yahweh as well. However, the text delineates several contrasts. In surah 112, the Arabic word *ahad*[4] stands alone and is translated as "is One", but Muslims understand that "One and Only" embodies all occurrences of "One" in reference to Allah. Yusuf Ali's translation demonstrates the word *ahad* as "One and Only" to reinforce this understanding. Consider what a Pakistani writer implies by the Arabic word, one (*ahad*).

"The Qur'an introduces us to two special attributive names of God that relate specifically to God's absolute oneness. These names are *Ahad* and *Waahid*. While in general terms, *Ahad* and *Waahid* could loosely be translated as 'One,' but more specifically, Ahad can be translated as 'One' and *Waahid* as 'Only.' Hence, when the Qur'an informs us that its Author is *Ahad* and *Waahid*, essentially what we are being told is that God, in the absolute sense, is the 'One and Only.'"[5]

For the Western reader, using transliterated Arabic words stands out and implies how important the Arabic meaning is to Muslims. The definitions convey absoluteness within oneness, forming unique aloneness. The one-and-only idea (*waahid*) idea also translates as *one* in Surah 2:163: "And your Allah is one Allah! There is no god but He; He is the Beneficent, the Merciful." (Shakir).[6] He is without another, altogether alone in his oneness. These two Arabic words summarize Absolute Oneness using *Tawhid*, a widespread term.

Surah 112:2 reads, "Allah is He on Whom all depend," further defining Allah's nature. Since he stands apart and alone, any imaginings of holding his hand or leaning on his breast dishonor him. Instead, dependence here pictures lowly mortals seeking mercy from the ultimate power since Allah is lofty and distant in contrast to a personal relationship. However, mercy in Islam becomes an important concept because all but one Surah begins with the *bismillah*,[7] part of

"Oneness implies perfection, and partnership signifies imperfection." Al-Tamimi, a Saudi Arabian scholar

which describes Allah as most gracious and merciful. Adherents learn *bismillah* to invoke a closeness despite Allah's distance in their lives. Despite the lofty distance, his mercy, without any indwelling presence, consoles the followers.

Allah does not beget, nor is he begotten.[8] Surah 112:3 stands in contrast to the God of the Bible, who declares Jesus his "Beloved Son." Allah's exclusive oneness does not allow another. The Ahmadiyya movement in Islam[9] strongly stresses the oneness of Allah. A key writer for the movement said, "Since God [Allah] is the only Being who is absolutely absolute in all respects, it, therefore, follows that in the absolute sense, there is none worthy of being sought but Him, there is none worthy of being worshiped but Him and there is none worthy of being loved but Him."[10]

The Quran rejects the idea of oneness in the unity of persons. Al-Tamimi, a Saudi Arabian scholar, states, "Oneness implies perfection, and partnership signifies imperfection."[11] Partnership as a keyword in Islam carries a negative connotation when associated with Allah since any partnership implies another outside of Allah as a rival. In light of these ideas, Allah's oneness is an Absolute Oneness.

Biblical Oneness in the Trinity

The Word of God shows that the Son and the Holy Spirit neither contend in rivalry nor create a partnership with Yahweh but demonstrate perfect harmony. The oneness of Yahweh consists of divine persons, not partners. The Jordanian Christian scholar Imad Shehadeh clarifies, "Divine persons, although there is distinction between persons, there is no separation, so that they share one and the same essence, and the existence of one person is eternally interdependent on the existence of the other person."[12] These divine persons form one essence, without partners. Each is distinct to enable eternal love between them but avoid rival partnerships, which Islam counters. So, though Christians know that Yahweh has no partner, followers of Absolute Oneness believe we have a corrupted version of Allah. In their opinion, we added persons or partners to their deity's aloneness. A.W. Tozer summarized, "The doctrine of the divine unity means not only that there is but one God; it means also that God is simple, uncomplex, one with Himself. The harmony of His being is the result not of a perfect balance of parts but of the absence of parts . . . He does not divide Himself to perform a work but works in the total unity of His being."[13]

Oneness in Unity describes the co-essence of persons within the Godhead. Oneness in Unity (Trinity) expresses divine persons' co-existence within the Godhead that maintains oneness and harmony. As will be evident, I am stressing the word "unity" more than what Christians may usually promote to highlight the uniqueness of biblical oneness in the divine persons and later the unity in a covenant marriage. Oneness describes the joining of persons, while unity describes the bond which holds the oneness together. Even though with God, the Oneness and Unity have always been from eternity past.

10

Consider the foundational verse on the oneness of Yahweh: *"Hear O Israel: The LORD*[14] *our God, **the LORD is one**. You shall love the LORD your God with all **your heart** and with all **your soul** and with all **your might**."* (Deut. 6:4–5; also, Mark 12:29–30). The LORD is one, yet he allows connection to the believer's heart and soul. The closeness centers on "The LORD our God," in which Yahweh enables believers to claim a nearness by expressing "our God." For believers, the LORD our God comes close to those who believe. Even within himself, a unity of person forms, called the Trinity, defining the divine persons' unity of the Father, Son, and Holy Spirit in oneness.

Furthermore, the key Hebrew statement begins, *"Hear O Israel: The LORD our God, **the LORD is one**."* This statement starts with "Hear," which is *shema* in Hebrew, becoming the *Shema*, the Jewish confession of faith. This statement centers on belief in Yahweh, and the word "one" becomes quite important. The Hebrew word for one is *"ehad,"* from which the Arabic word "ahad" comes. However, the context of both becomes quite essential.

The Hebrew text does not use the idea of Absolute Oneness to describe Yahweh's oneness but gives space for a plurality within that oneness. In Gen. 2:24, the phrase "one flesh" uses *ehad* to describe this becoming one flesh, a unity formed by the husband and wife. The Jewish mind would understand using "one" to define the unity of two persons. Despite the Jewish rejection of the oneness of Trinity today, "one" in this passage limits any sense of absoluteness when describing Yahweh. This plurality is also evidenced in the

Oneness in Unity avoids isolation; Absolute Oneness guards it.

creation of Adam and Eve when the Scriptures say, *"Then God said, "Let us make man in our image, after our likeness"* (Gen. 1:26). Unity defines the relationship more than any semblance of absoluteness.

The Difference in Oneness

Absoluteness contrasts with unity. Absoluteness demonstrates completeness in how Allah is one without any other persons. Unity, however, reflects the joining of persons. The Bible and Quran clash since Yahweh avoids complete aloneness in his essence, while Allah does not have any internal unity of persons. Their Oneness demonstrates how each willingly shares or holds back themselves. We are partakers of his divine image in creation, and Yahweh desires to connect with us. Later chapters will reveal how believers also enjoy unity with Christ in salvation and the indwelling Spirit in sanctification – all demonstrating a partaking of his divine nature. Oneness in Unity avoids isolation; Absolute Oneness guards it. One could say, for the absolute-oneness-concept deity: "The deity," with no allowance to attach personal pronouns. At the same time, the Oneness in Unity allows relationship by using the phrases *our God* or *your God*. The door opens for connection because he shares unity with himself and extends this to followers. In these key texts, the pronouns or lack of pronouns (Deut. 6 and Surah 112) formulates the contrast. Both are one, but Allah is one alone, while Yahweh's oneness intends to connect.

Quite often, when we lived among those who believe in Absolute Oneness, they questioned us, "Do you believe in one or three gods?" The question's importance for Middle Easterners ties the basis of belief with their concept of Allah as the one and only. My typical personal response was, "God is one, and he loves us." Thus affirming a key idea while creating a thirst for Yahweh's desire to connect with each of us. Christians never believe in three gods but must assert the belief in God's oneness more often without denying the Trinity.

Surah 9:31 states, "They have taken as lords beside Allah their rabbis and their monks and the Messiah son of Mary, when they were bidden to worship only One Allah. There is no Allah save Him. Be He Glorified from all that they ascribe as partner (unto Him)!"[15] Islam typically accentuates absolute oneness to counter Christianity. "If Allah had willed to choose a son, He could have chosen what He would of that which He hath created. Be He Glorified! He is Allah, the One, the Absolute" (Surah 39:4).[16] Allah categorizes absolute oneness with no son, partner, or likeness. In biblical thinking, the Lord Jesus as the eternal Son is never considered created or a choice to become a son, as this Surah presupposes.

When speaking of God as Trinity in Central Asia, the "threeness" of the word stood out more than the oneness[17] becoming a glaring obstacle to sharing the truth. In the Middle East, believers use an Arabic word for Trinity,[18] and confusion ensues. There will always be misunderstandings and natural resistance when explaining the Trinity to Muslims because the Quran presents the Christian truth as a false doctrine. Al-Ghazali, a prominent and well-known Islamic philosopher stated, "Oneness is the indication of the true, multiplicity is the indication of the false."[19] Thus, Al-Ghazali would say the Trinity is heresy. For these reasons, in Central Asia, I began to stress the essence of Yahweh's oneness during my initial conversations with our neighbors and friends, which helped them better understand what the Bible—not the Quran—says about Yahweh—likewise, key theological terms described meaning, which, as a result, countered certain false beliefs. Theologically, the Central Asian Christians understood the meaning of specific words and clarified these situations. Today, in speaking with Muslims, we need to know what terms they are using and what they mean by these terms. The nature of the deities' "oneness" presents a contrast that determines a distinct perspective on marriage.

The Oneness of Yahweh shares in unity rather than partnering by distinct, separate parts.

Yahweh's oneness reveals a complexity. *"In the beginning, God created the heavens and the earth. ² The earth was without form and void, and darkness was over the face of the deep. And the Spirit of God was hovering over the face of the waters.³ And God said, "Let there be light," and there was light"* (Gen. 1:1–3). We see God, his Spirit, and his Word ("God said") functioning in unity to create. They relate without rival partnership in creation. Unity, not disunity, labels their essence and work. Muslims assume this unity is another deity or a partner to the true God. Yet, unity cultivates unity in personal being and function, never displaying an internal rivalry.

The Oneness of Yahweh

Scripture shows us elsewhere that God and His Word are united: *"In the beginning was the Word, and the Word was with God, and the Word was God. He was in the beginning with God. All things were made through him, and without him was not anything made that was made... ¹⁴ And the Word became flesh and dwelt among us, and we have seen his glory, glory as of the only Son from the Father, full of grace and truth"* (John 1:1–3, 14). In eternity past, the Word existed, and the *Word was with God*. This Word was with him but also *was God*. Creation displays his ability to function in unity. This unity continues on display in John 1: the Word became flesh—God became flesh. The mystery of unity now adds the dimension of incarnation.

Oneness that Shares

In the creation of man, other hints of unity are evident. *"Let us make man in our image, after our likeness."* (Gen. 1:26) Yahweh shares his nature while maintaining unity—as Oneness in Unity or a Trinity in Oneness. He is one within himself and in perfect unity. He can share his *image and does so with humanity* without losing any unity.

"And when Jesus was baptized, immediately he went up from the water, and behold, the heavens were opened to him, and he saw the Spirit of God descending like a dove and coming to rest on him; and behold, a voice from heaven said, 'This is my beloved Son, with whom I am well pleased'" (Matt. 3:16–17). The unity of oneness is Father, Son, and Spirit. They never occur in modes like Father, Son, then Spirit but exist in persons functioning in oneness and perfect unity, without contention. He is beyond human understanding, uniquely one. God can speak from heaven about his beloved Son and send down his Spirit without fear of separation, rivalry, or domination. His will and movement are one.

The New Testament continually links God the Father and Jesus the Son as the one and only God. Paul says by inspiration, *"Therefore, as to the eating of food offered to idols, we know that 'an idol has no real existence,' and that 'there is **no God but one**.' For although there may be so-called gods in heaven or earth – indeed there are many 'gods' and many 'lords' – yet for us there is **one God**, the Father, from whom are all things and for whom we exist, and **one Lord**, Jesus Christ, through whom are all things and through whom we exist"* (1 Cor. 8:4–6.). The text presents the unity of the Father and Son as Lord and Creator to show a harmonious relationship that includes the Holy Spirit. We, as Christians, never see Jesus as another god competing against the Father, nor as a divine partnership. The mystery in oneness defines the one and only God of the Bible.

In English, the word "one," as in "we are one nation" or "the husband and wife are one," implies a unity of persons. In the same vein, I prefer to call the Father, Son, and Spirit a "Oneness in Unity" when beginning to teach about the richness of the Godhead to

14

promote oneness without excluding the divine personhood. True, oneness and unity can display redundancy in meaning, but *Oneness* describes the biblical emphasis that we believe in one God, not three. At the same time, *Unity* focuses on the united bond of distinct persons within that oneness—the Oneness of Yahweh shares in unity rather than partnering by distinct, separate parts. The descriptors Oneness in Trinity or a Trinity of Oneness highlight oneness rather than the threeness affirmed by the term Trinity. Knowing one's audience seeks to understand the context and how to affirm the oneness of the Trinity best.

Oneness that Loves

God's love (Yahweh) affirms the eternal relationship of the Godhead. Love cannot exist without another person because love expresses care toward another. The theological idea that *God and all attributes of God are eternal* includes his love. In Yahweh's eternal love, another must exist in eternity, a thought impossible in Absolute Oneness. C. S. Lewis said, "All sorts of people are fond of repeating the Christian statement that 'God is love.' But they seem not to notice that the words 'God is love' have no real meaning unless God contains at least two Persons. Love is something that one person has for another person. If God was a single person, then before the world was made, he was not love."[20] Thus, the triune Godhead's love between the unified divine persons flows out to others, encouraging and affirming relationship with himself.

Oneness that Saves

The Bible clarifies that God the Father (Yahweh) works in unity with his Word (Jesus, John 1:1–4) and his Spirit. The Scripture avoids a rival association in the Islamic sense where one is greater and the other lesser, despite their divine roles. Instead, they unite in essence. The Lord Jesus states, *"I and the Father are one."* (John 10:30). This inspired text equates God our Savior with the Lord Jesus as one in essence. Yet some would say the meaning here promotes only oneness in purpose, not of persons. Unquestionably, God and Jesus were one in purpose in the salvation process (10:27–29), but the hearers understood something greater in the context. In verse 31, we read that the Jews picked up stones, considering Jesus blasphemous when he equated himself with God. They testify in verse 33 to this understanding, *"It is not for a good work that we are going to stone you but for blasphemy, because you, being a man, make yourself God."* Even *a good work* like oneness in salvific purpose connects them, but for these Jews, the blasphemy of oneness, in essence, stoked their emotions.

Another passage further demonstrates Jesus's oneness as savior God, *"This is good, and it is pleasing in the sight of **God our Savior**, who desires all people to be saved and to come to the knowledge of the truth. For there is **one God**, and there is **one mediator** between God and men, the man Christ Jesus, **who gave himself as a ransom** for all, which is the testimony given at the proper time"* (1 Timothy 2:3–6). The Trinity of Oneness demonstrates a beautiful mystery because the mediator is Jesus as God/Savior. He is fully and truly God, as well as entirely and truly man, revealing himself as the intermediary between the Father and humanity. Only God saves, and these verses above affirm that even this oneness in purpose sources from their oneness in essence.

This great salvation grants a partaking of God's divine nature. Believers who share in his nature never lessen his wholeness; instead, he invites them to participate and share in God's nature. The New Testament affirms God *"has granted to us his precious and very great promises, so that through them you may become partakers of the divine nature"* (2 Peter 1:4). Through salvation's promise and God's power, the partaking unites us mystically to his divine nature. Partaking is an already-but-not-yet concept for believers in Christ. This joining with him evidences victory over the corrupted world along with an anticipation of a full partaking in the resurrections. The covenant partakers are those who participate in God's creative work. In creation, humanity partakes of his divine image; in salvation, believers unite with Christ; and in sanctification, the Spirit of God indwells—all demonstrating a sharing of his divine actions.

The Aloneness of Allah

The Unity of Yahweh contrasts with the Aloneness of Allah. Islam affirms that Allah has no partner, is not begotten, has no one co-equal or comparable, and is not like his creation. His aloneness without division excludes unity since the idea of "unity" unites and joins things together. The aloneness excludes persons and excludes a personal connection with creation. Therefore, the aloneness of Allah marks how Islam describes him.

Allah alone, without a Spirit

One sweltering day on a balcony in Queens, in discussion with some Muslim friends, I mentioned that God is a Spirit. From my viewpoint, I assumed this idea of a Spirit aspired to something both religions could readily agree on. After my statement, I remember quite distinctly their response: "If Allah is a Spirit or if Allah is not a Spirit, I do not know. He is one." I initially thought that if they did not know God was a Spirit, how could they know how he functioned? These recalled words evoked compassion as I realized their knowledge of God limited any deeper discussion.

In Allah's singularity, he has no partner or rival; thus, he has no spirit. When a Christian stated that *God is a Spirit*, the website "Islam Question & Answer" responded, "The Spirit or soul is not one of the attributes of Allah, rather it is one of the things that have been created by Allah. It is mentioned in conjunction with Allah in some texts by way of honouring, for Allah is its Creator and Sovereign, He takes it (in death) whenever He wills and He sends it whenever He wills."[21] Islam never describes Allah as a spirit. In Islam, the phrases: "He is alone," "he has no son," and "he has no Spirit" characterize Allah's singularity.

Alone without personhood

Typically, Islam avoids using the words "person" or "character" to describe the attributes of Allah. This lack of personality parallels Allah's lofty singularity. The Canadian Islamic scholar Jamal Badawi said, "For Muslims, monotheism does not mean simply the unity of God because there can be different persons in unity. Monotheism in Islam is the absolute Oneness and Uniqueness of Allah, which precludes the notion of persons sharing in Godhead."[22] Jamal Badawi prefers the word "absolute oneness" over the word which prefers the biblical view of "persons sharing in Godhead." His word choice contrasts with the biblical view because Islam does not promote persons when related to Allah's essence. Allah does not share his nature with anyone since no relationship exists within his nature.

17

Allah has attributes without personhood because the sense of personhood creates an association in Muslim perception. For this reason, Islam does not use the same terms we do. Allah has attributes that can demonstrate a moral value while avoiding personhood.

Absolute Oneness promotes a form of singularity without persons or partnerships. His distinct aloneness displays a lack of relatability and sharing.

Crucial points of Divergence

Muslims are required to believe in Absolute Oneness, which Amjad M. Hussein explains concerning the Islamic creeds: "To believe in God as is stated in the first article of faith means to negate any other deity and affirm the belief in the oneness and uniqueness of God, Who is the only One Who can be worshipped."[23] Their belief in Absolute Oneness limits and discourages exploring what the Bible promotes.

Let's consider what occurs without this trinitarian love between the Father, Son, and Holy Spirit. First, a non-trinitarian deity, like Allah, would need to create another person to love because no other person exists to love within himself. Secondly, Allah's divine power dominates his will without inner love, so his actions are driven by power and will, not necessarily by love. Therefore, his power creates distance and loftiness, resulting in a will that promotes submission.

The Christian idea of a believer's salvation resembling a partaking expresses an impossible truth in quranic thinking since Allah's nature has no partners, associations, or partakers. Furthermore, the terms differ in that Islam accuses Christianity of assuming the Trinity divides, or partners but these ideas do not represent the biblical viewpoint. For clarity, the view of the Trinity does not include any sense of modalistic form.[24] His essence is unseparated yet manifested distinctly by sharing himself in multiple ways in Scripture. As a unity of divine persons, the Trinity allows a sharing of self with humanity. The relational Yahweh interacts with his creation, which we will further study in the coming chapters.

As seen, Yahweh allows relationship, connection, and a joining of divine persons, while Islam positions Allah to be alone, with no other, and no uniting of persons. Allah does not co-anything, while Yahweh's unity reveals the divine relationship.

However, apparent exclusivity appears within both systems: Islam states that giving Allah a partner is one of the greatest sins (*shirk*), which is the sin of associating any partner with Allah's oneness. For them, rejecting the view of absolute oneness and accepting something different is categorized as unbelief. Likewise, Christians must accept Jesus as the Way, the Truth, and the Life and his concluding summary on how to come to God when he said, "No man comes to the Father *except through me*" (John 14:6). In both viewpoints, the apparent exclusivity makes the blasphemy of one religion the foundation of another. These exclusive markers become the initial openings for both yet close the door for the other.

Often, my Central Asian friends wondered if I believed in one God or three. They pre-supposed that someone either believes in Absolute Oneness or commits *shirk*. They desired to know where I fell in these two extremes. Truth be told, I do not believe in an Absolute Oneness God who is so alone that he is without personhood. Nor do I admit Yahweh within himself has rivalry or partnership. In mystery, I believe and worship the Triune God.

Connecting Marriage to Oneness

In this chapter, the bedrock of Yahweh's Oneness in Unity reflects what I believe is a profound similarity to marriage. The Trinity's oneness parallels the two-becoming-one principle of marriage. Whether in the Trinity or marriage, biblical oneness implies a mystical unity of persons, forming a harmony between distinct persons. Furthermore, in a covenant marriage, the divine presence centers the relationship to reflect a loving God.

Likewise, the ideas of Islamic contract marriage absorb the foundation of belief about Allah's Oneness. The essence of Islam promotes followers to seek their proper place in the Islamic community's obligations. Thus, the contract marriage never reflects any form of Absolute Oneness. The married couple comes together as partners, a quality not connected to Allah.

The actions of Yahweh and Allah will align with their natures. Their unique qualities compel them to act in specific ways; these set the tone for how they can reveal themselves. How do an Absolute

Oneness deity and an Oneness in Unity deity communicate with their subjects? The next chapter will explore this question.

For further study, see my blog's teaching tips concerning the Oneness of God.

Summary Chart of Oneness

Meaning of Oneness	Yahweh	Allah
Oneness	Trinity of Oneness	Absolute Oneness
Keywords	Unified – One	One and Only
Unity	Unity of Persons	Alone and Exclusiveness
Relational Aspect	Relational Divine Persons	Divine Reality – no Personality
	Encourages Relationality	Denies Relationality
Essence	One in Essence	Alone in Essence
Likeness	Bestows likeness	Free of any similarity or likeness
Issue of rivalry	Shares without rivalry	No associate rival possible

Chapter 2 - Indwelling Inspiration or Divine Download?

"Then Yahweh stretched out his hand and he touched my mouth, and Yahweh said to me, 'Look, I have put my words in your mouth.'"
– Jeremiah 1:9 – (LEB)

Besides our many letters, much of my wife's and my dating experience consisted of walking on the streets of London. We planned to visit the British Museum one day, and I recall two pictures I took of my wife-to-be. In one, she posed near the ancient images of the Ishtar gate of Babylon, which Daniel would have seen. But on the other, she stood near the famous Rosetta Stone. This historical find was among the first bilingual artifacts to unlock Egyptian history. The stone decree revealed how the Greek language deciphered the two hieroglyphic texts, a key to understanding hieroglyphics.

Rosetta Stone refers to unlocking essential clues to an area of study. For Christians, the sacred book is the Bible; Islam's text is the Quran. The development of these texts will offer clues that define how Yahweh or Allah communicates to their followers.

The distinct communication patterns observed in Yahweh and Allah indicate that Yahweh promotes a relational indwelling inspiration while Allah presents a complete dictation from above.

The Bible and the Quran existed within contexts that promoted either a covenant or contract interpretation. For our purpose, we ask how and why these books came into existence. Is the process of revelation in both narratives distinct or similar?

Two Ways to Communicate

The Persian teacher and I had just taught three classes about the Word of God. We explained the beauty and importance of the Word in our lives, focusing on how the Word of God came through inspiration. The Bible speaks the very words of God, given through the prophets by inspiration. After three classes, I thought I would ask whether God's Word descended or was inspired. Because of my background and assumption that we had clearly taught the subject matter, I confidently thought all would affirm the inspiration of the

Word. Thus, I felt no need for debate. Yet these believers from a Persian Shia background struggled and debated the point, with the majority claiming surely the Scriptures came down. Despite our assumed understanding, we realized the students' presuppositions were in play. Many in and near the Middle East think that the Word of God came down verbatim from above—a process devoid of inspiration.

For Sunnis and Shiites, the coming from above is the exclusive delivery direction. Let's explore why these distinct ideas matter for believers in Christ and give us a better understanding of how God communicates. Much like the distinct oneness of deity, these sources flow from deity's nature since each distinctly uses an appropriate means to communicate—Yahweh indwells, and Allah remains above. Much like his own relationality, an oneness-in-unity deity will seek to relate closely in giving his communication. Still, an Absolute Oneness deity will maintain his lofty position, allowing only downward communication. Both communicate consistently with their covenant or contract nature.

Two analogies are before us:

1. The Oneness in Trinity reveals from within or near to the messenger through inspiration. His communication methods encourage a personal, horizontal manner in delivery.

2. To avoid association, the Absolute Oneness deity reveals from above, not from within. His communication method displays only a vertical impersonal manner.

What is Inspiration?

"The Spirit of the LORD speaks by me; his word is on my tongue."
2 Samuel 23:2

Did God's Word descend down or was it inspired by the Spirit? And the students' response motivated me to rethink how inspiration took place and, especially, how to teach it. I realized that etching my presupposed ideas into the hearts of believers from a non-Christian background is not an easy chisel. For example, Persians use the biblical word *revelation,* but I did not realize how they might define it differently for many years.

We looked at our new group's translated version of a doctrinal statement in a church planting situation with a Persian pastor. We changed some words and then made a wall poster of the main statements of faith. After a few months, the Persian pastor said, "We need to remove the word *revelation* and replace it with the word *inspiration.*" He said the former word would create misunderstanding for new believers, who would think God's word came down. I wondered, *Revelation or inspiration, are they not the same thing?*

In light of this, we changed the doctrinal wording in the original statement to reflect biblical inspiration rather than descended-down understanding. Despite these changes, we continued to display the older version on a poster. After some time, an elder from another church visited our group since there was talk of churches merging. He complimented the poster and loved that the church displayed its teachings. *However,* he said, *I do not like the word 'revelation' in the statement about the Word of God.* His statement confirmed our previous point of concern. For believers in an Islamic context, clarity becomes crucial. In Islamic understanding, revelation describes the downward method, but in the biblical perception, God's revelation comes to us in an inspired manner through various forms.

Indwelling Inspiration is the God-breathed process in which the Spirit of God generates the very words of God through or intimately near the messenger. The inspiration process mysteriously breathes through the personality of the messenger.

Only 2 Timothy 3:16 uses the biblical word *inspiration,* "All Scripture is inspired of God." This important passage translates a Greek term that, etymologically, means "breathed out by God."[25] The passage parallels another text which says the Spirit carries the prophet along to write the words of God (2 Pet. 1:19–21). Inspiration presents a God-breathed mystery with the prophet to generate an act of breathing out the very words of God. The Holy Spirit breathes, mysteriously generated within or near the messenger or even a personal from-above experience on a few occasions.

Interestingly, the proper noun, *Scripture (graphe),* found here assumes the recorded material by God to include every portion of the

Word of God by making an emphatic claim in the wording—*the Scripture from God is breathed by God.*

During the Old Testament days, the Spirit of God randomly indwelt the people of God, but consistently God's presence resided in their midst. Interestingly, Isaiah 63:10–11 states, *"But they rebelled and grieved his Holy Spirit; therefore, he turned to be their enemy, and himself fought against them. Then he remembered the days of old, of Moses and his people. Where is he who brought them up out of the sea with the shepherds of his flock? Where is he who put in the midst of them his Holy Spirit."*

Even the Spirit during these days could be grieved as if he indwelt them, yet his dwelling presence was in their midst. In many portions of Scripture, the inspiration's place remains a mystery. The prophet Micah alludes to the indwelling Spirit for inspiration, *"But as for me, I am filled with power, with the Spirit of the LORD, and with justice and might, to declare to Jacob his transgression and to Israel his sin"* (Micah 3:8). The prophet, empowered with the filling of God's Spirit, spoke the words of God by breathing out words to declare God's will and intent. The focus on communicating the very words of God depicts Micah's close encounter with Yahweh.

Prophet's Participation

Without hesitation, the Bible depicts the message coming from God with the messenger fully interacting in the process. The passage **Indwelling Inspiration is the God-breathed process in which the Spirit of God generates the very words of God through or intimately near the messenger.** in 2 Pet. 1:16–21 amplifies the inspiration process, *"For we did not follow cleverly devised myths when we made known to you the power and coming of our Lord Jesus Christ, but we were **eyewitnesses of his majesty.** For when he received honor and glory from God the Father, and the voice was borne to him by the Majestic Glory, 'This is my beloved Son, with whom I am well pleased,' **we ourselves heard this very voice borne from heaven,** for we were with him on the holy mountain. And we have **the prophetic word more fully confirmed,** to which you will do well to pay attention as to a lamp shining in a dark place, until the day dawns and the morning star rises in your hearts, knowing this first of all, that no prophecy of Scripture* *comes from someone's own interpretation. For no prophecy was ever produced by the will of man, but men **spoke from God as they were carried along by the Holy Spirit**"* (bold mine).

The voice of God from heaven confirms the prophetic words bestowed on the *beloved Son* and heard by the disciples who were present. God reveals himself and comes near with his majestic glory. The God of the Bible is near, often evading distance. He shares his glory, and the recipient can sense it. His emotions display his feelings for his beloved Son. He verbalizes approval, and the disciples hear these words of affirmation and love. Even though from above, the process shows God's nearness in a highly horizontal format. The voice came from above to Lord Jesus, but the text says, "We were with him" to create nearness, in that they heard God's active declaration. He speaks and brings down his glory to the very presence of the disciples. Peter testifies, along with the other disciples, how biblical revelation and inspiration blend, forming what I call *participant inspiration.*

Spirit Inspiration

In Christian theology, the Holy Spirit becomes the main actor for inspiration. Contrary to Islamic thinking, the Scripture says, *"As they were carried along by the Holy Spirit"* (2 Pet. 1:21). Picture a sailboat moved along by the wind. Similarly, the Holy Spirit personally moves the hand of the messenger to create scripture. God and the messenger were fully involved in the process, yet the Spirit controlled the process in a relatable, intimate manner. Participant inspiration marks a Spirit-led revelation.

In the inspiration process, God's messenger experiences a carrying *along by the Holy Spirit* to produce Scripture by God's will, not by a human hand. A Christian apologist, Dan Wickwire summarizes that the Bible "is just what it is designed to be, namely, a homogeneous, uninterrupted, harmonious, and orderly account of the whole history of God's dealings with man. The Bible is not such a book a man would write if he could or could write if he would."[26] The Bible originated from God. Yet, the human messengers fully participated in the inspiration process *"as they were carried along by the Holy Spirit."*

Biblical inspiration stands unique in the ideas of religious revelations. The biblical scholar Warren Wiersbe affirms, "We must not think of 'inspiration' the way the world thinks when it says, 'Shakespeare was certainly an inspired writer.' What we mean by biblical *inspiration* is the supernatural influence of the Holy Spirit on the Bible's writers, which guaranteed that what they wrote was accurate and trustworthy . . . *inspiration* has to do with the *recording* of this communication in a way that is dependable."[27] Divine inspiration involves the Holy Spirit speaking through the prophet of God to write an eternal, unchanging word. The Spirit's supernatural process never manipulates like a soothsayer or similar to poetic feelings produced. Earthly poets write from their heart perspective, but God's Spirit sources biblical inspiration without the messengers' private perspective (2 Pet. 1:19–21). Thus, biblical inspiration marks a unique way God's Spirit created Scripture.

Points of Clarity

A few points need clarity concerning the inspiration process:

1.   Inspiration describes the overarching idea of how the Word of God came about yet includes various methods to demonstrate God's relatability. He delivers his message in a fashion consistent with his character of relationality. In any relationship, creativity in communication varies, but the essence of inspiration portrays relatability. God's creativity in inspiration includes but is not limited to the use of dreams, visions, stone tablets, prophecies, conversational dialogue, stories, and writing on a wall. Poetic inward inspiration and revelations from above encompass the mysterious process.

2.   Inspiration demonstrates the relationality and closeness of Yahweh, eliminating the possibility of a detached, distant deity who only gives a dictate to recite. Inspiration manifests his dwelling presence in the lives and context of Spirit-filled people. Defining God-breathed inspiration implies intimacy and closeness.

3.   Inspiration reveals progressively, along with divine decrees, God himself. God, in his inspired words, reveals his will and himself to humanity.

Defining Progressive Revelation

Progressive revelation labels God's act of incremental disclosure in revealing himself, his will, and his truth with new revelation, which always complements and supplements what has come before. The Scriptures unfold to reveal more about God and espouse an ever-deepening knowledge concerning his plan. The sixty-six books of the Bible show God to be relational, close, and desirous to connect with humanity. Progressive revelation affirms that every later revelation by another messenger enhances and validates what was before. So, if a messenger comes and tries to replace or invalidate a previous revelation, then this messenger's actions can be questioned as not being from God.

The Chicago Statement on Biblical Inerrancy in Article V affirms and summarizes the point:

*We **affirm** that God's revelation in the Holy Scriptures was progressive. We **deny** that later revelation, which may fulfill earlier revelation, ever corrects or contradicts it. We further deny that any normative revelation has been given since the completion of the New Testament writings.*[28]

R. C. Sproul, a signatory to the statement, further explains, "The Bible is to be regarded as a holistic book in which the Old Testament helps us understand the New Testament and the New Testament sheds significant light on the Old Testament."[29] The fully inspired Word of God interconnects Genesis to Revelation with a progressive revealing flow concerning who God is.

Progressive revelation does not abrogate

Any person working with Muslims needs to understand that in Islam, Allah reveals a one-time manuscript to the messenger, which denies any semblance of progressive revelation, yet at the same time, Islam promotes a concept called abrogation. For this reason, I give more detail than expected on this subject since the main issues of difference depend on progressive revelation.

When encouraging my Middle Eastern friends to read the Bible often, I hear what I call "the later-greater" theory. Often, Muslims greet discussions about the Bible with *Oh; I respect and reverence all the books Allah has given — the book of Moses, David, and the Injil (New Testament) of Jesus. But now we have the final revelation in the Quran.*

28

Despite never having read the Bible, they dismiss the Scriptures based on this later-greater theory. Fear stifles them even when they become willing to read these past divine books. The later-greater theory teaches the complete finality of their book and the abrogation of past books.

Abrogation is the Islamic concept in which a later quranic text replaces an earlier text. This process alters the former meaning or ruling to become an authorized cancellation procedure within Islam. In Islamic practice, their current book abrogates or replaces the former books of the Bible. This means that the former books become useless to their present faith, and subsequently, they refuse to read them. However, at the same time, they place other non-heavenly books above Scripture, like *al-Tabari's History* and Ibn Katheer's *Stories of the Prophets.* These Islamic historical writings survey biblical stories and give each one an Islamic bent. Often, these books are readily available to buy in their Muslim societies.

The later-greater theory ignores progressive revelation. Much like Mohammad Hamidullah, a scholar of Islamic Law, states, "All the revealed books deserve to be treated with utmost respect and reverence. I do not act on all the books but only on the last one—the Qur'an—on the principle that the latest order supersedes and abrogates the earlier ones."[30] The last book superseded the former, so in this Islamic theory, a Muslim verbally affirms the Bible but ignores reading the inspired words. Since Islam discounts progressive revelation, our teaching must include biblical progressive revelation to affirm the permanence of the Bible.

Their perspective redefines respect and reverence. If I were a guest and the host said he respected and admired me but did not listen to me, nor even let me speak, I would have misgivings with the host's affirming words. Similarly, their profound respect for their book and prophet motivates them. For them, *the latest order* is all they value and grant any consideration. Yet they prohibit their *former* books from speaking, abrogating them so that Muslims will not read them. As a host to their former *revealed books*, Islam offers only disrespect to these guests, granting no influencing seat of honor but expecting silence.

As mentioned before, the concept of revelation in Islam encompasses both the process and the product. The Islamic download stored in the download folder becomes ready for the installation of submission. Their assumed all-inclusive revelation denies any previous Scripture. However, for the Christian, the product includes all the God-breathed Scripture of the Bible. They respect the books of Moses and David and believe in the usefulness of the Old Testament for today. No abrogation or superseding exists since the purpose of God's word reveals the author and specifically the Lord Jesus Christ. Thus, the Bible shows a received, completed product for believers.

The idea that the last book supersedes the former books ignores the storyline of the Bible. As the remarkable storyteller, Yahweh desires to woo us with the extraordinary story of salvation. Abrogation ignores the gospel seeds in the narrative of Adam and Eve, especially the promised seed to Abraham in which the provided lamb of God instead of Abraham's son points to the future Savior. The later-greater theory tramples upon these gospel seeds and sows weeds among them. For Christians, the medium is the message. The way God speaks throughout history demonstrates his interactions with humanity. If one ignores the medium of progressive revelation, then the message changes, which the abrogation method does. Islam changed the fundamental nature of how one views the giving of the Word of God, along with any progressive revealing of God himself.

> **Progressive revelation does not just join parts but joins prophets together to proclaim the same message in an ever-widening and deepening way.**

Progressive revelation tells a different story than the one which abolishes the former books. Furthermore, the abrogate-narrative changes the story of salvation. On the surface, all seems the same, but the narrative changes the ethos of the message. As Christians, we know God's inspired narrative takes priority over any other religion's storyline.

Unfolding of Revelation

In other words, progressive revelation does not just join parts but joins prophets together to proclaim the same message in an ever-widening and deepening way. No part of revelation excludes or abrogates another prophet since inspiration unifies what came before. Islam promotes a replacement revelation process, mistakenly thinking their book supersedes what came before. Replacement never honors or respects God's eternal words because replacement would make God's word temporary and open to annulment. The unfolding of biblical revelation results in a unified inspiration process that continually allows God's ancient words to speak to us today.

Jesus warns against one prophet abrogating another and any allowance in limiting the manner of progressive revelation:

"Do not think that I have come to abolish the Law or the Prophets; I have not come to abolish them but to fulfill them. For truly I tell you, until heaven and earth disappear, not the smallest letter, not the least stroke of a pen, will by any means disappear from the Law until everything is accomplished. Therefore, anyone who sets aside one of the least of these commands and teaches others accordingly will be called least in the kingdom of heaven, but whoever practices and teaches these commands will be called great in the kingdom of heaven." (Matt. 5:17–19, NIV).

The Lord Jesus stresses the eternal nature of God's Word—not one item of the Scripture will disappear—affirming the unity of the Bible. The Jews, during the time of Christ, were setting aside the Word of God and allowing another authority to replace it. They honored tradition or interpretive phrases to affirm external practices without internal change (Matt. 5:21–48). In light of this, Christ warns about the false sense of honor of those who set aside the Word of God and claim another authority.

The idea of setting aside means to annul or dissolve "the Law or the Prophets"—an apparent reference to the past Scriptures. The Lord highlighted "least of these commands" to counter a Jewish thought process that defined commands as either "light" or "heavy." The Jews thought the lighter commands could be ignored. By countering this idea, Jesus emphasized the permanence of the unity of the Scriptures so that even defining a command in the least category takes away from the durability of the Scripture. The New Testament scholar Leon Morris comments, "As the words about teaching men show, the attitude condemned is one of doing away with the commandment in question, regarding it as nonexistent, as null and void. Even to nullify just *one* commandment is serious."[31]

Despite Jesus not directly talking about the Islamic abrogation process, the intent of the Jews seems similar. The Lord Jesus condemned any form of abrogation. Those who teach such things will be called "least in the kingdom of heaven" (Matt. 5:19). Dishonor comes to those teachers who void the Word of God, but to read, practice, and teach the whole counsel of God opens the path of greatness in the kingdom of heaven.

The scope of abrogation — avoiding the well-spring

I love to give portions of the Bible to others in their native tongue. On a visit to a mountainous area of Central Asia, I, along with other staff members of a relief agency, enjoyed the hospitality of an older gentleman. The village was known as *Fresh Well* since the center had an artesian spring that bubbled out, forming a small stream of water that flowed alongside the road. This respected man was genuinely kind and honored us with a meal. At the time of departure, he headed to the fields to herd the cattle to drink from the spring.

As we were leaving, I wanted to give him the New Testament (*Injil*) in his native tongue. I lifted the book for him to see and said; *This is the book of Jesus. I want to give you a gift.* He replied, *Oh, we have our book, including all we need, and we have those stories in our book.* Realizing his intent to reject our book, I should have stopped there since Islam warns against reading the *Injil*. But the author of the book prompted me to say, *This book is the well-spring, the source of the stories of Jesus. Much like this village, if one wants to drink from the well-spring, do they go to the opening or below the spring? This book is the well-spring source. The source of the life of Jesus, wouldn't one want to read that?* At that moment, maybe because of honor, he took the book. He handed the book to the daughter-in-law and motioned it into the house. He then left to go to work. After he left, the daughter-in-law turned to us, smiled, and said, *Oh, I want to read this book; I had a dream about Jesus.*

The Bible is God's unchangeable, unabrogated, and non-replaceable Word. The God-inspired well-spring nourishes our souls today. So, let us drink from the spring of God's Word.

Progressive revelation reveals God himself
"The LORD continued to appear at Shiloh, and there he revealed himself to Samuel through his word." (1 Samuel 3:21, NIV)

The Scriptures give us a light to know who Yahweh is, revealing and communicating knowledge about his person as well as his book. A Palestinian Christian, Imad Shehadeh said, "The concept of the progress of revelation discussed earlier conveys that any information that God reveals about himself is based on or is consistent with what he earlier revealed about himself. So, in the beginning, God declared himself through nature, or General Revelation. He then revealed himself through the inspired Word, or Special Revelation, beginning with the prophets of the Old Testament and continuing with the apostles of the New Testament. The zenith of Special Revelation came in the incarnation."[32] These metanarratives reveal the Oneness in Trinity's heart, climaxing with the coming of the Lord Jesus. Yet the non-progressive revelation cancels these lofty ideas and closes the heart's door to know and dwell with the biblical God.

He further states, "One of the factors that distinguishes the solid foundation from the corrupt foundation is to what extent it is consistent with the progress of God's revelation of himself throughout history and through his prophets and the Holy Scriptures It will be seen that the right concept of God builds on the foundation of the previous progress of revelation in the Bible, whereas the wrong concept of God rejects the previous progress of revelation."[33] For this reason, we contrast the nature of oneness and see what each indicates in how they communicate. Yahweh's story indicates a lover who reveals and sacrificially gives, never denying what he previously said.

Meanwhile, Absolute Oneness retains his position of loftiness and respect by saying, "Recite!" Allah has a story of submission to download, ignoring a self-revealing potential. He stands alone, with no personal connection except utilizing a book from above. One can know about a great historic character in history without really knowing the sound of his voice, the feelings he once had, and the way he interacted. Similarly, quranic notions indicate a grand "reveal" that reveals no person but a contractual submission, depending on commands without sufficient ability to know or create intimacy. The medium of Islamic revelation continues the idea of a detached deity, far from a lover in pursuit.

Narrative of Self-disclosure

Progressive revelation allows for the story narrative to unfold. His care for humanity, his pursuit to deliver them, and the coming of God himself as the savior—all delineate his loving-kindness and concern. In the garden narrative, he pursues and demonstrates love, where he clothes a sinful Adam and Eve. The Lord continues with the pattern of sacrifice, providing the ram for Abraham, then establishing the sacrificial system of Moses and a promised sacrificing savior, which Jesus fulfilled. He sacrificially gave himself to redeem humanity. Little by little, God's plan discloses elements of surprise and suspense. The core narrative revealed God himself and the continual self-sacrificial pursuit of his people. Yahweh's love still desires to dwell in oneness with those who believe. He woos and sacrifices to dwell with us, depicting the eternality of the relationship (Rev. 19,21). The Word of God reveals a plan with divine decrees to know a sacrificial savior that differs from knowing only a messenger.

God divulges his great salvation by dropping seeds of truth, along with prophecies of hope, to bring about a blessed promise. As the master artist, God draws the narrative picture because he pursues and willingly sacrifices for his beloved. These themes demonstrate the benefit of a progressive revelation for the biblical narrative.

Yahweh reveals himself progressively over multiple centuries through biblical inspiration. His Spirit dwells near and breathes the very words of God through the mouth and hand of the human messenger. He allows participation and comes alongside even to indwell the messenger. Out of necessity, his nature communicates horizontally while affirming vertical respect and obedience.

Narrative in Revealing Will

In contrast, the Absolute Oneness deity reveals a will to obey, avoiding personal revealing of himself. Abdullah Saeed mentions that Islamic revelation disallows making Allah known but only his Will in a comprehensible language.[34] Allah reveals his will, decrees, and guidance[35] but not himself. He may turn his face toward humanity, or they may sense he is as close as their jugular (Surah 2:115), yet the issue of self-reveal remains questionable. A turned face may initiate disclosure, but the interaction stops there. For the Muslim, the face turned, and the closeness to the jugular vein aligns their awareness with doing his will. Self-revealing is not the focus, but instead, submitting to Allah's will.

Muslims misunderstand the idea of biblical inspiration since their text refuses

> Yahweh draws the curtain aside to reveal a finite view of himself, while Allah draws the curtain tight and will only reveal his Will.

to reveal Allah himself but only his will. Inspiration opens the door to God's intended closeness, but Islamic spectator revelation does not. The systematic theologian Fred Sanders offers, "The doctrine of Scripture and revelation is uniquely important because it prepares the ground for anything we want to say in the entire field of theology. The reality of God is that he can only be known if he takes the initiative to be known."[36] The God of the Bible does that. He takes the initiative to be known by revealing himself. In contrast, Islamic thinking disallows an initiative for Allah to self-reveal as he maintains a power distance with Muslims. In summary, Yahweh draws the curtain aside to reveal a finite view of himself, while Allah draws the curtain tight and will only reveal his Will. Their respective paths of revelation demonstrate these distinctions.

Islamic Revelation

Islamic word *wahy*[37] means revelation, a direct reveal of the Quran from above, given orally. The word functions as a divine download upon the messenger without any participation of the messenger. This purposeful disengagement reveals Allah's will, avoiding self-reveal in his person. Let's search deeper to see what Islam says about revelation.

From above, not from within

First, the idea of Islamic revelation sources *from above*, not *from within*. The oft-repeated Arabic word *tanzil* [38] portrays the *from above* idea as the act or transfer of the message from heaven to earth.

(Surah 15:6–10; 17:105–106). Many English translations[39] translate *tanzil* as *reveal* but leading Islamic scholars[40] translate the word more specifically *sent down*, which describes the Arabic more accurately.

Affirming the Islamic idea that their book came down upon their prophet, often described as *the advent of the Quran*.[41] This advent is often highlighted and remembered during the month of fasting as *the night of power*. In this sense, the word *tanzil* gives direction from heaven to earth as a keenly vertical movement.

Upon, not through the prophet

The quranic process of revelation is generally described as *upon* the prophet, not *through* the prophet. Imam Abu Hanifa states, "The Qur'an is the speech of Allah Most High: written in texts, memorized by hearts, recited by tongues, and *revealed upon* the Prophet"[42] (italic mine). The reveal from above grants the understanding that Islamic revelation can only come upon the messenger to exclude any inner awareness. Some scholars describe the process with the words "without fragmentation"[43] so their messenger, "who accordingly was assigned the task of passing on the verses verbatim,"[44] will avoid a relational involvement in the process. The messenger's task was to recite the verses given (Surah 2:129, 2:151; 3:164), which the word "say" repeated over 300 times in their book, proving a verbatim emphasis.[45] The upon-ness revelation enables their deity to remain above to further a sense of awe in his remoteness. Thus, the revelation came upon the messenger and never through indwelling the messenger.

Downloaded, not progressive

The Islamic revelation process transports down an entirely composed text to limit the possibility of an inner or inter-agent transaction. Such a process makes their revelation exclusive but not inspired. Haleem, the London Islamic scholar, emphasized this point by declaring the use of "other forms of the verbs *nazzala* and *anzala* ('to send down') occur over three hundred times in the body of the Quran, again stressing the fact that it has been sent down from God and is His direct Word."[46] His essay in the appendix of Nasr's *The Study Quran*, along with another essay about the Quran, avoids using the word "inspiration" even once to describe the process. Without much debate, Muslims do not represent the Quran's revelation in any connectable form like biblical inspiration.[47]

In Islamic thinking, the total product of revelation equates to a downloaded package given to their prophet over twenty-three years. For them, progressive revelation includes *only* these twenty-three years, avoiding the definition of biblical progressive revelation. Sure, they state Abraham and other Old Testament saints submitted to Allah, but the placement of these historic individuals into an Islamic understanding counters any semblance of progressive revelation. Often, in Islamic literature, the context of these individuals supports a quranic narrative, adding statements concerning them that ignore the biblical narrative.

Furthermore, Islamic writers use the word 'revelation' to include the process as a product. For them, Allah revealed both without any separation between the process and product. They have excluded any relational steps and only described the outcome as coming down. In biblical understanding, revelation describes the product, but inspiration the process. Limiting the process enables Islam to avoid an inspirational link with Allah and the messenger. He reveals a product, and the messenger receives the outcome. The download comes upon the messenger to tell verbatim the book.

Revelation without the Holy Spirit

How does an Absolute Oneness deity reveal a message? Since Allah is not a spirit, he cannot inspire humans. The Islamic explanations state he can only let down his word; he cannot, in the biblical sense, dwell with or in humanity nor use a divine Spirit in this Islamic process. If Allah duplicated this method, he would accept an association or a partnership, committing *shirk*. He instead gives from above his text to humanity to maintain his alone oneness and loftiness. Therefore, an angel mediates the Islamic download: "Rather, the Quran—that is, its component parts—were 'sent down' from 'heaven' in oral installments by the divine messenger identified as 'Gabriel'—the angel of revelation throughout human history—and received by a willing human receptacle."[48] Gabriel often stated as a spirit becomes the carrier of the installments downloaded.

In our new believers' class at the Persian church, the lesson centered on the Holy Spirit. Over a few weeks, this topic covered the many beautiful roles of the Holy Spirit, including the Spirit's role in communicating the Word of God and salvation. As we were wrapping up the discussion about the Holy Spirit, a lady raised her hand and asked, "Is the Holy Spirit Gabriel?"

Despite being surprised by her question, I instantly thought of many Persian poets like Hafiz who mentions the Holy Spirit and his influence on the heart. The question related to their culture, so I asked, "Why would you think this?" The dear lady alluded to the link of Gabriel to the process of Islamic revelation. The view of a downward revelation highlights this *angel of revelation* as the virtual private network to connect the source with the message. They believe that contract revelation is received *without* the Holy Spirit yet often utilizes an angelic spirit to speak to their messenger. Let's explore the Islamic understanding of "spirit" a bit more.

Comparing the definition of "Spirit"

The Quran talks about a spirit (*ruh*) providing the means for their book, though it never equates this spirit with the Holy Spirit of the Bible. Surah 42:52 says, "We reveal to thee an inspired book." (Shakir) or "Thus have We revealed unto thee a Spirit from Our Command" (Nasr). The Arabic word translated as "inspired" or "spirit" is *ruh* and quite crucial to their teachings. A quranic Ahmadiyya commentator suggests, "The use of the word *ruh* ('inspired Book') as meaning inspiration, and not the soul, is conclusive here. The Qur'an is called the *ruh* or the spirit because it gave life to a dead world."[49] Despite incorrectly using the Christian term *inspiration*, this *ruh* is not the divine Holy Spirit but a way to define Islamic revelation. The term *ruh* enables them to describe the influence of the Quran without an inner aspect. Nasr affirms, "In the context of the previous verse, *a Spirit from Our Command* can here be understood as a reference to the Quran."[50] This spirit labels the revelational process and influence but never affirms the biblical idea of the Holy Spirit.

However, some attached *ruh* to the angel Gabriel to describe how the Islamic revelation came down, often called a holy spirit in Islamic circles.[51] When they speak of the *Spirit*, they mean Gabriel. The Islamic creed of Imam Abu Ja'far al-Tahawi confirms in creed #89, concerning the Quran, "which the Trustworthy Spirit (*Jibreel*) came down with." *Jibreel* (Gabriel in English) is the angelic spirit they believe relates to Islamic revelation. His presence, sometimes explained as the angel of revelation, displays a more leading role than the messenger himself.

In conclusion, the Islamic *ruh* is not the Holy Spirit since they believe Allah dwells alone in his absolute oneness. So, the word *ruh* could mean life-giving influence or a reference to Gabriel. The clarity in "spirit" is crucial because the revelatory process of both *sacred* texts involves a spirit—one divine, the other not.

Participant Inspiration	Spectator Revelation
From God's Spirit	From Above
With the Messenger	Upon the Messenger
Horizontal relationship	Vertical to Maintain Loftiness
Reveals Yahweh Himself	Reveals Allah's Will
Progressive Disclosure	One-time Download
Unified Inspiration	Absolute Dictation
Reveals Yahweh's Essence	Concealed Allah's Essence
Curtain drawn aside	Curtain closed tight

Contrast Revelation and Inspiration

To say the Islamic word for revelation and the biblical word for inspiration are the same is too simplistic, yet often, these terms intermix in many comparative studies of Islam. Yahweh and Allah speak, but their natures define how they will communicate. Allah evades inspiration-like interaction with the messenger because Muslims believe their revelation existed previously, so Allah only needs to dictate his words. Yahweh, never tied to a verbatim form, works differently. He desires to come alongside, work through, and inspire the heart of his image-bearer to bring forth his word. Their manners of communication reveal their distinct natures of oneness.

Logically, this study analyzes two significant belief systems and what each says about itself. However, the inspired Word of God, the Bible, is truth. John C. Whitcomb, Jr. stated, "If Christianity is merely a circle of truth which is conditioned and defined and judged by other circles of truth, then it is not a 'truth circle' at all; for the Scriptures boldly and consistently claim to be God's eternal, all-inclusive, unique, final, and thus absolutely authoritative Word."[52] We are blessed to have God's truth. The supposed sameness between the Bible and Quran projects a façade. The Bible marks how to know a covenant-related deity. In contrast, the other uses the "truth" to formulate a seeming parallel alternative.

Two clarifying points:

1. in their understanding, Islamic revelation precedes from above upon a detached messenger. Conversely, in biblical inspiration, the Spirit breathes inwardly within or near the messenger, moving him to write the very words of God. The one carried along by the Spirit forms a mystery alignment between God's Spirit and the prophet, contrasted with the Islamic thinking that promotes a purposeful disengagement.

2. Islamic scholars use the word "revelation" but not necessarily "inspiration." However, both terms are evident in biblical writings yet defined differently than in Islam.

Absolute Dictation vs Relational Inspiration

Islam emphasizes the life of their messenger as a part of the religious path, but the method of revelation tells another story. Their revelation comes in dictation so that their deity maintains absolute control in his communication as he offers a mandate for adherents to recite.

Muslim authors convey dictation occurs without a personal role:

- "The standard Muslim view of the Revelation *does not allow any role* for the Prophet Muhammad in the genesis of the Qur'an, the total composition of which Islam attributes to *God alone*, fiercely rejecting any idea that supports human involvement. God is the sole 'author' of the Qur'an and Muhammad's role is reduced to that of a *recipient* of the sacred text and *transmitter* of it to his people."[53] (Abdullah Saeed, italic mine)

- "The Qur'an is the word of God; the Speech of God (*Kalam Allah*) verbatim."[54] (Ghulam Haider Aasi)
- "The task of the Prophet-Messenger was only to utter a discourse revealed or unveiled to him by God as part of His uncreated, infinite, co-eternal Speech."[55] (Mohammed Arkoun)

These statements portray that verbatim dictation defines the revelation process. The strict exactness in the words of these authors attempts to minimize the messenger's role while affirming Allah's fundamental role. For this reason, I call the Islamic revelation process *Spectator Revelation* because the messenger resembles only a passive *recipient*. He receives the process like a spectator, without participation. From Allah's lofty position, he distributes the verbatim message to the messenger by means appropriate to his nature of aloneness. Verbatim ensures no co-participation and no partnership, just *the speech of Allah*. Allah is alone in this Spectator Revelation, ignoring the mystery of inspired participation found in the biblical viewpoint.

"Verbatim" recalls rote learning, a method of repetition. The meaning of the Arabic word "Quran" means to recite, which encourages repeating word for word. Islamic revelation reveals the contractual religion so submission can occur. How their revelation came about is inconsequential; instead, they prioritize absolute submission. In a submission context, relationship, indwelling, and personal connection with Allah often become secondary concerns to maximize the need for submission and fear.

The absolute oneness of Allah does not allow another in partnership since his loftiness keeps him distant in communicating vertically from above. His contractual nature maintains a position by only granting an angelic spirit to come near for the dictated session.

Direction of Communication

Yahweh and Allah are, by nature, distinct in their oneness and how they communicate with their adherents. One desires proximity and the other distance. In considering the direction of inspiration, the

God of the Bible allows intimate, full participation with the messenger, while Allah maintains loftiness in a come-down format. The former communicates horizontally, but the latter only vertically, so these two different religious sources lead to different inferences. Participant-Inspiration and Spectator-Revelation mirror their deity's manner of oneness and character.

In textual archeology, clues reveal facts about those who wrote the artifact. The clues in the religious texts of the Bible and Quran disclose how the author communicates. The Egyptian Rosetta Stone also hints at how the king of the second century wanted to communicate before the birth of Christ. He chose three languages to mark his decree. To create political unity, he tried to communicate this decree in the classic, local, and trade (Greek) languages.

Interestingly, the Bible has three languages: Hebrew, Aramaic, and Greek. As common everyday languages, they granted people an understanding of God's message. The desire for clarity echoes in the many efforts to translate the entire Bible into about 700 languages and the New Testament into over 1500 additional languages.[56] The decree in the Rosetta Stone intended clarity. It later enabled many linguists to study hieroglyphics, so likewise, the Bible allows us to know God better and opens the door to reflect on his greatness.

The textual search for our study indicates the personality of Yahweh, who draws as near as possible to the messengers by progressively giving his words of communication to reveal himself. However, the other, Allah, maintains a distance and allows an angel to disclose his decrees to establish a mandate of submission. These communicative methods further define how deity will create humanity. Will they maintain their distinct essence in their actions? How near or distant will they make the object of their communication? Then, the principles of human creation will open the door to their deliverance and how to live.

Revelation's Connection to Marriage

The progressive process of biblical inspiration reveals a relatable God who comes close to his people. Likewise, covenant marriage displays two people committed to communicating together. Covenant intimacy draws each side together to know and be known. The mutual sharing between them creates deeper intimacy.

Inspiration depicts how God makes himself known in a self-revealing manner. Likewise, each spouse needs to self-reveal their desires, concerns, needs, and thoughts to build a more profound intimate proximity with their spouse. God reveals himself in his word; likewise, covenantal couples need to share themselves to provide light to each other's needs and desires. Intimacy is to know one's spouse and to be known by one's spouse. A marriage relationship moves from the unknown to the known, desiring personal revealing to encourage continued growth in closeness.

The Word of God progressively reveals a plan along with his divine decree. In the same sense, intimacy in marriage needs a progressive plan to grow in intimacy consistently. Contrast that with the husband who told his wife at the wedding, *I love you,* and then years later always joked; I said, "I love you," and then *if I change my mind, I will let you know.* Intimate knowing never becomes a one-time event or declaration but is progressive in discovering more about one's spouse through the seasons of life. Similarly, believers can grow closer to God progressively as they read and meditate on the Word. The living Word expects growth in intimacy from believers, much like each spouse hopes to experience in a Christian marriage.

Inherently incompatible with the revealing concept of intimacy is the contracted Absolute Oneness' will, which places on Muslims a guidance for life. This guidance is the innate Allah-given human enablement to lead them toward Islam. The Path of Islam lives out in their marriages. In the same way, a revealed will empowers contract marriage more than revealing one's self. The husband reveals his will, and the wife submits to him. The Islamic messenger received the message, passively becoming only a recipient of the dictated text. The Islamic revelation process dictates more than self-discloses. Therefore, Islamic contract marriages absorb this passivity since the husband dictates more than self-reveals. The Will of Allah revealed requires submission. The contract ethos disregards the necessity to self-disclose to create deeper intimacy.

See my blog for tips on teaching Inspiration in a Muslim context.

	Participant Inspiration	Spectator Revelation
Definiteness	The Spirit	A spirit
Channel of Communication	Holy Spirit	Gabriel
Direction	Personal presence with	Coming down upon
Words	Fully inspired	Verbatim
What is revealed?	Self-revealing of Yahweh	Revealing Allah's Will
Progressive Revelation	Essential	Non-progressive
Intent	Covenant Dwelling	Contractual Submission
Role of Abrogation	Disallows Abrogation	Allows Abrogation
Action of Messenger	Active	Passive

Chapter 3 – Image Determines Purpose

There are no ordinary people. You have never met a mere mortal – C.S. Lewis[57]

The trap was set. The religious leaders of Jesus's day sought to snare him concerning money. Would he favor the government or God? Would he deny a much-despised practice of paying taxes? They questioned him about money and favoritism, but the Lord Jesus's response clarified the meaning of life.

They started: *Teacher, we know that you are truthful and do not care about anyone's opinion. For you are unswayed by appearances but truly teach the way of God …*

Then, the seemingly entrapped question comes: *Is it lawful to pay taxes to Caesar or not? Should we pay them, or should we not?*

The mighty Roman government officials looked on to see what this religious figure would say. Knowing that many Jews did not pay taxes, would he fuel the fire of non-compliance?

Quite aware of their intent, Jesus responded: *Why put me to the test? Bring me a coin, and let me look at it.*

What? Everyone knows what the Roman coin looks like. Maybe the coin was a ploy to pay the taxes.

The religious leaders gave him a coin, most likely a tiny denomination. He then asks *The coin depicts whose likeness and inscription?*

Simple enough, thought the religious leaders: *Caesar's.*

The Lord Jesus, knowing the Scriptures and the purpose of life, says, *Render to Caesar the things that are Caesar's, and to God the things that are God's.*

They stood speechless![58]

God designed his image-bearers to belong to and connect with him in a relationship. Belongingness means we live for him and worship him, rendering unto God what belongs to him. We are God's—we belong to him, imprinted with his image. Our life, our body, and our very existence belong to Him.

Christian theologian Erickson connects this belongingness with relationship: "The image of God is universal; it is found in all humans at all times and places. Therefore, it is present in sinful human beings. Even in turning away from God, one cannot negate the fact of being related to God in a way in which no other creature is or can be. There is always a relationship, either positive or negative."[59] No matter your current view of God, we all bear our Creator's image.

Covenant and Contract Reflections

Humanity's creation reflects a purpose-driven paradigm consistent with Yahweh's or Allah's character. The Bible shows Yahweh creating humanity in his image to form a divine-human relationship. Still, the Quran presents Allah maintaining distance, without a shared image, to instill a guidance upon humankind.

In the previous chapter, we saw that the nature of the sacred books imitates the essence of oneness. Yahweh values participation and involvement to portray his quality of relationality, while Allah seeks to guard his elevated position. In the creation of humanity, we will continue to see the *divine* tendency in which Yahweh will actively participate in the creation of humanity, and the Absolute Oneness deity will maintain a semblance of detachment.

In this ancient search for meaning, the biblical image of God motif will provide a pivotal find to promote relationship. The question before us to consider is: what are the consequences of a faith that promotes humanity in God's image and one that does not? Our chosen paradigm will influence how we view ourselves, especially our spouses. Is the husband the image of a loving steward to collaborate with his wife? Or is the husband the image of a ruler to control his wife? This chapter will define the different outcomes of the creation of humanity, especially the roles depicted as either an image-bearer or a vicegerency.

The Spirit's Nearness

In Creation, the God of the Bible involves himself via his Spirit. From the beginning of Genesis, the Spirit of Yahweh hovers over the waters of the earth (Genesis 1:2). He dominates over creation yet intimately connects to it. K. A. Mathews, an Old Testament scholar, said, "The movement of God's 'Spirit' indicates that the creative forces for change commence with God's presence."[60] His presence is apparent, and he creates by speaking.

The Spirit motif demonstrates his interactive closeness. The verb *hovering* implies attention like a bird caring for her young, indicating that the Creator's Spirit intimately cares for the creation he speaks into existence. The German commentator J. P. Lange conveys this idea, "The Spirit of God is the unity and life-motion of the creative divine activity."[61] God the mover is ready to deal with creation intimately. Unmistakably, the start-up message reveals that the Trinity of Oneness intimately and consistently involves the divine self in the creation process by depicting his Spirit hovering over and dwelling near the water. His active presence in an intimate display of unity establishes the world.

Allah's Loftiness

In contrast to Yahweh dwelling with his creation, Allah remains exclusive above creation. The Saudi scholar Al-Tamimi highlights this fact, "Thus, the Muslims singled Allah out, described Him with Attributes of Perfection, Elevated Him above all attributes of imperfection and exalted Him from attributes of His creation being like Him."[62] Al-Tamimi continues, "One must also possess unequivocal convictions that the attribute [*Tawhid*] is at such a level of perfection, nobility and loftiness that it cuts away at all that gives rise to erroneous impressions of similitude between Allah and the Attributes of His creation."[63] For a Muslim, to create an impression of similitude is an error, and the follower of Allah must avoid the association at all costs; thus, no *erroneous impressions* attach to the Creator. Dwelling with Allah is not an option but keeping him elevated is.

An Islamic website promotes this separateness: "It is worth noting that the basic message of Islam is that Allah and His creation are distinctly different entities. Neither is Allah His creation or a part of it, nor is His creation Him or a part of Him."[64] Both perspectives (Bible and Quran) avoid pantheism, but Allah's disconnect from Creation, at times described as aloof by some Christians, does not describe their attitude about God. Allah's above uniqueness and his unknowability create a distinction that Islam continually attempts to maintain. For Muslims, Allah's approachableness connects to his revealed Will, which suffices for them to know. Similarly, the exalted Yahweh Creator intends to be above yet near his Creation. His nearness distinguishes him, while Allah's loftiness excludes him from being a *part of it.*

These images of the Spirit's nearness and Allah's loftiness display choice nuggets in our search to understand how each creation account resembles their nature. Their closeness or distance infers divine purpose to the biblical or quranic narrative. So, let's dig deeper as we explore how the creation of Adam differs in the biblical and quranic accounts.

Creation of Humanity

Spirit Breathing Creates Man

The biblical Creator intimately formed man: *When Yahweh God formed the man of dust from the ground, and he blew into his nostrils the breath of life, and the man became a living creature*[65] (Gen. 2:7, LEB). The Word of God speaks other parts of creation into existence, but this scene gives more of an intimate focus. Yahweh, the potter, shapes man and then breathes life into him, connecting intimately. The scene instills discomfort as the scene moves beyond the divine potter's hands to center on his breath and mouth. Like an intimate scene in a movie, the audience emotionally moves with uneasiness or excitement when God moves close to breathe life. The nostrils, a more natural place to breathe in than the mouth, receive the life-breath of God to live.

The God of the Bible consistently comes alongside to remove distance. He shapes Adam, breathes life into his nostrils, and as a living creature lifts him. Soon after, he speaks the marriage description to Adam and Eve to heighten closeness. Yahweh, the lover, grants this identity to Adam. The biblical narrative spotlights intimacy in initiating creation. As we will see, the Quran's central theme focuses on man's position as the vicegerent, which does not necessitate closeness.[66]

Despite the boundaries on Adam and Eve in the garden, the Creator Yahweh abides near them to evidence continued consistent care and interaction. Surprisingly, even in the aftermath of sin, Yahweh is there, asking Adam and Eve about their sin. He does not avoid the problem but enters the emotional aspects of the separation. Despite his holiness, he cares. Sin separated them but still, his loving concern remains. As the judge, Yahweh will punish but also listen as an advocate. When sin takes hold of the hearts of Adam and Eve, Yahweh relates and eventually restores the lost fellowship. His actions consistently reflect an intimate, caring relationship.

Spiritless Creation of Man

"Who made all things good which He created, and He began the creation of man from clay; [8] Then He made his seed from a draught of despised fluid; [9] Then He fashioned him and breathed into him of His Spirit; and appointed for you hearing and sight and hearts. Small thanks give ye!" (Pickthall, Surah 32:7–9)

Despite Surah 32:9's affirmation, as we have seen, Allah does not have a Spirit. This phrase repeats in Surah 38:72, which Islamic commentators link to demonstrate Allah's creative power to give life. The Canadian Islamic scholar Philips explains, "The claim that God is a spirit or has a spirit completely ruins this area of *Tawhid*. Allah does not refer to Himself as a spirit anywhere in the Qur'an nor does His Prophet express anything of that nature in hadith. In fact, Allah refers to the spirit as part of His creation."[67] For Allah to be spirit would establish a partnership that minimizes his Absolute Oneness. Philips suggests that the spirit is a created part of Creation. The biblical Holy Spirit does not match this spirit appearing in the quranic creation account. In Islam, Allah creates a spirit to formulate Creation, again to keep himself at a distance. This spirit reflects the last chapter's discussion about the spirit

The God of the Bible consistently comes alongside to remove distance.

remaining either a life-giving influence or just a reference to Gabriel.[68] Islam grants no possible reference to a divine spirit being involved in the quranic version of creation. Allah speaks of Creation in his aloneness with no Spirit to accompany him. In archaeological evidence, ancient artifacts form categories and distinctions that cannot be ignored. Likewise, a Spirit-less Allah generates a distinct category that appoints a man to oversee his submission mandate.

Al-Ghazali, the 11th-century philosopher, claims Allah is utterly unique and alone as the sole member of Creation. To compare God to man, he says, "There can be no class to which God could belong lest God be considered one of a kind instead of the only one of His kind."[69] Allah is unlike anything—he allows no comparison or sharing. Al-Ghazali continues, "(One must) deny similarity (between God and the other things) absolutely."[70] Allah placed above man so that no characteristics will resemble him. If man resembles a particular action attributed to Allah, then this attribute in Allah is utterly unique and different from man. No sharing and no association of his oneness become possible; thus, Muslims categorize him as spiritless in contrast to the Holy Spirit in the Bible.

How will a spiritless Allah create? When the Quran states, "breathed into him of His Spirit," despite the capitalization of Spirit, this is not a divine spirit but only a giving of life.[71] To avoid the use of Spirit, more recent translations by al-Hilali and Khan (1999) correct this use by stating *soul* instead of spirit: "So, when I have fashioned him completely and breathed into him (Adam) the soul which I created for him, then fall (you) down prostrating yourselves unto him."[72] (Surah 15:29, al-Hilali). In the quranic account, Allah creates the soul/spirit by breathing or creating him into man; however, as proven, the spiritless Allah empowers creation without a direct breath from his mouth. The breathing of life seemingly exists like the biblical creation, but the scene of intimate closeness in breathing into his nostrils is absent.

Yahweh and Creation of Humanity	Allah and Creation of Humanity
God is Spirit	Allah creates spirit-like movement
Humanity as image-bearer	Man bears Guidance
Humanity rules over creation but as an Image-bearer	Man rules over creation as a Vicegerent
Created to relate to Yahweh	Created to submit and rule

Man, the Image-bearer of God

Yahweh communicates in how he creates and gives biblical inspiration. The Creation account indicates his nearness and willingness to share by stamping his image on humanity. However, the revealed Will of Allah does not leave a divine imprint but a divine contract-like mantle on humanity obligating submission, which becomes apparent with the Islamic Adam as a vicegerent.

Before we delve into the vicegerent motif, let's fully explore the meaning of man as the image of God since this key idea creates distinct biblical purposes.

Then God said, "Let us make man in our image, after our likeness. And le them have dominion over the fish of the sea and over the birds of the heavens and over the livestock and over all the earth and over every creeping thing that creeps on the earth."

So God created man in his own image,
in the image of God he created him;
male and female he created them.
And God blessed them. And God said to them, "Be fruitful and multiply and fill the earth and subdue it, and have dominion over the fish of the sea and over the birds of the heavens and over every living thing that moves on the earth." Genesis 1:26–28

Separate from Animals

The *image of God* motif description only applies to humans and never animals. However, if we look at biblical anthropology, we can see how humanity differs from animals. These differences offer clues to the meaning of this divine imprint upon humankind.

Potential qualities that hint at what the Image of God means:

- Intelligence
- Rationality
- Emotions
- Volitional will
- Consciousness
- Sentience (capacity to feel)

- The ability to communicate.[73]

The characteristics mentioned above vary in every human being's capacity. They distinguish us from animals without defining the image of God entirely since more distinct ideas will explain this concept. Furthermore, Islam thoughtfully accepts these same characteristics for humanity with some degree of difference.

Stewards of the Earth

In Gen. 1:26–28, the first human responsibility given is a dominion mandate over the world. While being made in God's image and given dominion over the earth are mutually exclusive ideas, both are true in the biblical account. The Quran affirms humanity's dominion, but it denies humanity being made in God's image.

The image of God in Adam and Eve marks a finished stamped identity without a necessary element of doing (dominion). Theologian Millard J. Erickson proposes, "The image is something in the very nature of humans, in the way in which they were made. It refers to something a human *is* rather than something a human *has* or *does*."[74]

However, to be fair, Michael Heiser explains that dominion is essential to the Creation account. "Being created as God's imagers means we are His representatives on earth—the only qualification for this is that we are human. This is why the creation of humankind as God's image in Gen. 1:26–27 is immediately followed by the so-called dominion mandate of Gen. 1:28. Humanity is tasked with stewarding God's creation as though God were physically present to undertake the duty himself."[75] Stewardship flows from their image-bearing. For these reasons, God's image gives them their central identity – life as image-bearers. The mandate following this granted them dominion and stewardship.

God Speaks His Mind

Let us make man in our image, after our likeness. Genesis 1:26

During a study of Genesis, after reading the above passage, an Iranian refugee asked, *Why is God speaking here? Why does he explain himself?* These questions intrigued me. God could create man and say,

Be! Nothing more needs saying. However, these few words, *Let us make man in our image, after our likeness,* convey a message, a purpose, a divine insight. The verbal Creator speaks and relates. We do not know if he said so specifically when he created angels, but he did speak creation into existence and added commentary about himself when making humanity. In this very intimate moment, he shares his thoughts with us, even allowing a bit of self-revealing. *Let us make man in our image, after our likeness.*

These intimate thoughts hint at who he is and who we are, paralleling our search into the essence of Oneness. The text in the Hebrew mindset may not prove a Trinity but hints at his essence and certainly conveys a potential nearness. *Let us, our image, our likeness,* pronounce a mutual connection. Creation forms new life, but even more so, formulates a relationship between the Creator and humanity. Yahweh shares and comes close by sharing his *image* and his *likeness.* This association or, as some would mistakenly say, "partnership" does not lessen who he is. When God creates, he is never less than himself. He neither changes nor can face rivalry by interacting or sharing. He is beyond human thinking. The assumed thought that an earthly monarch who shares or associates with a weaker or lesser person would lose honor, self-essence, power, or status is incorrect. Quite the contrary, the divine graciously sharing of himself brings honor. God speaks his mind — who are we *not* to take notice and stand in awe?

Image Connects with a Divine Spirit

The image of God shows that spirituality exists in humanity but not animals. What is an image? Image replicates or only copies the primary substance. To represent someone does not include exact replication but an imitated presence. Humanity replicates God spiritually in a finite way, avoiding a bodily image of the divine.

Man, made in God's presence, becomes a sacred image-bearer. Man has a spirit (I Thessalonians 5:23), and God is a Spirit (John 4:24). The image-bearing concept links as a reason not to curse or kill another (James 3:9 and Gen. 9:6). Humanity's identity includes the sacredness of life. Respecting others equates to respecting God. The image connection joins two spiritual beings more than a particular physical feature. The physical similarities between Adam and his children do not necessarily directly describe how humans bear the likeness of God.

Eternal Dimension

God is eternal, and so is the human soul. The inspired words affirm the infinite dimension when the soul passes into eternity: *we would rather be away from the body and at home with the Lord* (2 Cor. 5:8). The created body of Adam does not make him eternal, but the image-of-God dimension does. Furthermore, God *has made everything beautiful in its time. Also, he has put eternity into man's heart, yet so that he cannot find out what God has done from the beginning to the end* (Ecc. 3:11). God placed an eternal perception into the very core of humans, yet they remain finite in their understanding of God's ways. The infinite dimension of humanity links with the everlasting God; as C. S. Lewis correctly said, "There are no ordinary people. You have never met a mere mortal." Despite being mere mortals, we, in the eternal perspective, become potential channels for a lasting relationship with our Creator.

Divine Relationship

Digging in-depth into the human eternal dimension and a possible divine relationship, the scripture says, *"So God created man in his own image, in the image of God he created him; male and female he created them."* (Gen. 1:27). The divine relating includes Adam and Eve—*male and female*—since the Scriptures say both possess his image. In these verses, the meaning of the word *man* describes both the male and femaleness of humanity. Even more instructive is that the term "image of God" assumes a divine and human relationship. The Creator who speaks and shares his mind simultaneously conveys the purpose of life—to connect to the Creator.

Erickson affirms the focus on relationship, "The image of God is not to be understood in terms of any structural qualities within humans; it is not something a human is or possesses. Rather, the image is a matter of one's relationship to God; it is something a human experiences. Thus, it is dynamic rather than static."[76] The divine relationship continually pursues relationship, never static, despite the lack of pursuit from humanity at times. One may ask, why stress such a simple concept? Those from an Islamic background are well aware of obligations, rights, pillars, and external means to be *spiritual*. Biblical spirituality displays a different bedrock that roots the image-of-God concept to visibly highlight the interactions between God's Spirit and our spirit (Rom. 8:12–17). In the Islamic setting, *spirituality* means the external religious façade, but biblically, a spiritual person connects to the Spirit in an internal heart relationship.

As a deity who values relatability, Yahweh gives the ability to relate to humanity. The creator/image-bearer relationship **Humanity created to dwell intimately with God prioritizes over any sense of ruling in power for him.** displays the preeminent focus that humans reflect the Creator. Still, they rule and steward the world like their Creator from this image-of-God relationship—male-and-female-in-our-image ushers in unlimited possibilities of connectedness. Humanity created to dwell intimately with God prioritizes over any sense of ruling in power for him. The Creator does not say: *Let our power, enable man in our rule and our likeness to dominate.* A power emphasis would convey the vertical purpose of ruling and subduing the world, but this focus is a secondary concern. Relatability cultivates an identity more than occupation. For those consumed with the power motif, these words need to sink in so one will focus more on being than doing.

The Creator marks a horizontal perspective—*Man-and-woman-in-our-image* depends on and connects to his Creator. The creator/image-bearer relationship displays the preeminent focus. Yes, humans are given dominion like the Creator, but they can only rule and steward the world like their Creator if they connect with the image-of-God relationship. Without the divine-human connection, work and ruling become meaningless. In the verbal thought of the Creator, the text focuses on the relationship since the *image*-motif sandwiches the *dominion* concept in Genesis 1:26–27. The divine-human link meshes, establishing a dwelling together. However, the following verses mention the earthly function of humanity—to care for the world around them. Humans, as image-bearers, steward the earth.

The purpose of humanity is to love and dwell with God. From God himself: "Hear, O Israel: The LORD our God, the LORD is one. You shall love the LORD your God with all your heart and with all your soul and with all your might. And these words that I command you today shall be on your heart" (Deut. 6:4–6). The divine relationship remains primary over all others. Much like the Lord Jesus declares, *render to Caesar the things that are Caesar's, and to God the things that are God's,* God created us for divine relationship. We belong to him.

Man, the Vicegerent

The unknowable Allah cannot be known by his likeness. Al-Ghazali said, "What is utterly unlike what is known to man cannot be known."[77] This unknowability relates to his nature but, as previously discussed, Allah makes known his Will. For these reasons, no Surah in the Quran mentions Adam created in Allah's likeness or image. Furthermore, nothing in the Quran leads to a personal divine relationship on par with the biblical one. The quranic account defines Adam exclusively by his placement, countering the image-of-God print on the biblical Adam.

Considering the general placement of the quranic Adam clarifies how Islam views human deliverance and life. In Adam's quranic creation, he is not an image-bearer but identifies as a ruler, even over angels. His placement aligns with the submission mandate to rule while submitting to Allah's Will. Despite similarities in dominion, the quranic Adam's identity differs from the biblical Adam's.

What is a Vicegerent?

A keyword to describe the quranic Adam is vicegerent.[78] Understanding this term will clarify the perspective of Islamic anthropology since Adam is higher than the angels. Adam as a vicegerent, an empowered deputy to rule for Allah by enforcing submission to Allah. In a Central Asian theological class, I asked, "Who is placed higher, man or angels?" A fellow Central Asian minister, who often joked with me, chuckled, "What kind of question is that? It's such a silly question. Why are you asking this?" Apparently, the positioning of Adam is slight and subtle for Central Asians but with eternal consequences.

The Arabic word *Khalifa* describes the idea of vicegerent. A vicegerent establishes on the earth submission to Allah's rule.

Sometimes, *Khalifa* is translated as successor, deputy, or ruler.[79] According to the history of al-Tabari, one reason for this title is that Adam succeeds the jinn (supernatural spirits) on the earth to represent Allah's rule on earth.[80] Two firsts often parallel the *Khalifa* concept: the first human being and the first prophet. Vicegerent, translated from the Arabic word *Khalifa,* means one who stands in the place of someone else or, secondly, one who assumes the position of another.[81] The Islamic Adam replaced the supernatural spirits and took on a position to bring into existence those who follow Allah's guidance.

Issue of rank

The placed vicegerent of Allah has rank. In Surah 2:30, Allah says to the angels, "And when thy Lord said unto the angels: Lo! I am about to place a viceroy (*khalif*) in the earth, they said: Wilt thou place therein one who will do harm therein and will shed blood, while we, we hymn Thy praise and sanctify Thee? He said: Surely I know that which ye know not."[82] The text uses the words *to place a viceroy . . . thou place therein*. The idea of place and rank concurs with other quranic texts like Surah 6:165, which mentions viceroy and rank together, and Surah 15:28, which says Adam as a viceroy whom the angels bowed to (Surah 35:39). The quranic setting sets up a potential tension between Satan and the newly formed Adam when his presentation by Allah honorably places him above the angels.

With Adam placed above, everything else submits to him. Notice the lack of an Islamic woman recognized as a vicegerent. In the quranic account, the name of Eve is never mentioned and the tension between Adam and the angels does not connect with Adam's mate. So, for this reason, a scholar like Abdulati states, "Man also is created by God and commissioned to be God's vicegerent on earth. Man is so chosen to cultivate the land and to enrich life with knowledge, virtue, purpose, and meaning. And to achieve this goal, everything in the earth and the heavens is created for him and is made subservient to him."[83] Adam is a deputy to commission Allah's Will on earth. He, as vicegerent, gives succession to his descendants and represents the contractual placement of humanity in a rank above angels.

Al-Tabari's history covers vicegerency by highlighting two reasons for Adam's rank over the angels. His endowment instills him with knowledge and authority. First, this history mentions Adam's knowledge specifically since he names the animals and has the authority to enforce the Will of Allah. Secondly, the Islamic vicegerency enhances a ruling/dominion theme, particularly over the angels. These themes also exist in the biblical narrative but with a distinct focus. The Bible stresses a horizontal dwelling relationship resembling covenant thinking, while the Quran encourages a contractual above-below placement. These distinctions layers present evidence to demonstrate how Allah interacts, underlining the vertical order over any horizontal relationship.

Adam – the Islamic Representative

In the creation of humanity, the Bible stresses a horizontal dwelling relationship, while the Quran encourages above-below placement.

As vicegerent, Adam is the representative of all of humanity. Nasr highlights, "Although it is clear in the Quran that Adam also represents all of humanity—male and female—in the account of his original creation, his vicegerency, his Divinely granted knowledge, and the prostration of the angels before him . . ."[84] Nasr clarifies the importance of Adam as a representative to the embedded evidence that characterizes and empowers the contract submission. The extent of Adam's position (vicegerency), with guidance and placement above angels, strays from the biblical narrative. The guidance as the innate Allah-given human enablement grants an endowment by Islamic knowledge for all Muslims to overcome any sinful weakness or any concept of a sinful nature. The Islamic Adam represents the exalted guided man from heaven without the deity's image.

Adam, the contract-representation connects humanity by functioning for all Muslims. He, like Muslims, was endowed with divine knowledge to claim self-deliverance by submitting to Allah. The Absolute Oneness deity is ever-present but without dwelling within man. In the form of divine guidance, His Will directs humanity, but not his indwelling presence or Spirit. There is neither heart-eternality in this guided deputy but rather only the *divinely granted knowledge* tasked for earthly submission.

Placed above Angels

The Central Asia introductory conversation often went as follows:

Al-Salaam, How are you? Are you good?

Thanks, I am good. And you?

I am good and glad to meet you. I am Jon, and what is your name?

My name is Safar.

Oh, glad to meet you.

Surprisingly, the next question, more than not, was: *In what year were you born?* This unique cultural question inquired about my birth, ignoring my age. The new relationship tended toward rank and placement quite quickly. Stating one's birth year gave a social ranking that reflected the manner of introductions. From the get-go, the older person expects the younger to honor and prefer. So, *in what year were you born?* This question became the standard phrase to claim where we both stood.

Declaring a year was more definitive than stating how old a person is. Once, recollected at a Central Asia dinner how a woman was celebrating her 40th birthday and at her birthday party, the group discovered that she was quite a bit over that amount when she said the year of her birth. Her response was she wanted to celebrate with her friends again. Yet a date does not lie or change, so the birth year was always the defining point.

In what year were you born? The answer to the question placed the questioner and questioned into a Central Asian pecking order. Who is older? The older will identify as an older brother or sister out of respect, while the younger will comply. The initial greetings formulate placement. Likewise, the initial greeting between Adam and Iblis (Satan) did the same. Despite his late arrival at Creation, Adam ranked above Iblis in the Islamic narrative.

Allah introduces Adam to the angels, establishing their placements in the pecking order of creation, much like an honor-based society that values rank. A deity whose actions are contractual also tends to be concerned with placement. Adam's place becomes the lynchpin to the quranic narrative to affirm a contract deliverance.

Not only is the quranic Adam the representative and the source of authority for Muslims to seek submission along with Allah's mandate, but he becomes superior to angels. The question appeared directly online: *Is man superior to angels?*[85] The answer summarized: "This is the reason that we read in the Qur'an that when the Almighty Allah created Adam. He commanded all the angels to prostrate before him and ordered Adam to tell the angels what he knew and in other words Allah made Adam the teacher of the angels." Islam's focus on Adam's position over angels dominates the conversation. First, Allah affirms Adam's place by requesting the prostration of the angels. Then, Adam's knowledge of teaching them what they did not know placed him over them.

Adam's placement above angels differs distinctly from the biblical account. In Psalm 8:6–9, what Adam, or humanity, rules over defines the dominion:

"Yet you have made him a little lower
than the heavenly beings
and crowned him with glory and honor.
You have given him dominion over the works of your hands;
you have put all things under his feet, all sheep and oxen,
and also the beasts of the field,
the birds of the heavens, and the fish of the sea,
whatever passes along the paths of the seas.
O LORD, our Lord,
how majestic is your name in all the earth!

This psalm displays God's crowning and honoring humanity during Creation. Verses 6–8 affirm humanity's dominion over animals, beasts of the field, birds, and the underwater world. Yet notably absent is dominion over angels, which the Quran desires to emphasize. Psalm 8 qualifies his dominion as the earth under his feet but not including the realm of angels—quite an important distinction.

I would propose the following line of logic that results from this mandate by the Absolute Oneness deity as he places Adam above angels, endowed with authority and knowledge. First, the appointment aligns with a contract understanding of responsibility. In a contract, the responsibilities, obligations, and, at times, the authority of the signees are known and defined. Endowment often further describes a contract to guarantee or enable specific actions. Then Allah commands the angels to bow to Adam to further heighten his place as vicegerent, the greatest of Allah's Creation. Finally, Allah, a contract deity, honors Adam, aligning with how the Islamic relationship functions. The hierarchal rights and obligations of society mirror this episode. In discovering ancient pottery, the science of archeology attempts to define organic residue in the porous material. Adam's placement is a residue of the Islamic story, leading to further enhancement in the value of rank, position, and honor in their Islamic worldview.

Iblis Speaks His Mind

Iblis, assumed as Satan, is a title mentioned eleven times in the Quran.[86] Amazingly, nine of these times, the situation refers to Iblis's rebellion in refusing to bow to Adam at Creation. This episode, absent from the Bible, marks a core story of Islamic identity for humanity.

In Surah 15:29, Allah says concerning the creation of Adam, "*So when I have made him complete and breathed into him of My spirit, fall down making obeisance to him.*"[87] After the creation of Adam, Allah mandates angels to bow to him. Iblis then speaks his mind.

In Iblis's two-fold response, he thinks he is better than Adam in position and better created. He says, "I am better than he; Thou hast created me of fire, and him Thou didst create of dust" (Surah 38:76, Shakir).[88] The issue of rank—who is better or who has authority— becomes central. Interestingly, in this oft-repeated quranic account, the focus avoids Adam's personhood but centers on his power and position. Iblis's response assumes that he, as a creature made of fire, is higher than one made of clay. For our purposes here, this episode of Allah's vicegerent affirms the position of Adam as the deputy of Allah, empowered with responsibility. He is not Allah's image, nor a person whom Allah dwells with to develop a divine relationship, but he represents Allah's deputy even over the angels. The Islamic account manipulates the Adamic identity to defend and promote the Muslim manner of deliverance.

Bestowed with Guidance

The basis of the quranic Adam's position relates to the knowledge Allah gave. The Egyptian-born Hammudah Abdulati proposes this "knowledge that qualifies man to be the vicegerent of his Creator and entitles him to command the respect and allegiance even of the angels of God."[89] The knowledge qualifies all humanity to be placed as vicegerent, meaning *to command the respect* on earth and even in the angelic realm. As mentioned, Islamic thought believes the specific knowledge of Adam involved knowing the names of animals, of which the angels were ignorant (Surah 27:1–2). This theme evolved to include the idea of divine guidance for everyone in their literature.

Allah's narrative reveals his Will, not his person. The critical component of his revealed Will in the contract mandate of submission parallels the guidance endowed to Muslims. The Will depicts the program of Allah in the Quran, which demands submission. The guidance becomes a synonym for the idea of true religion. Shakir's translation states, "He it is Who sent His Messenger with the guidance and the true religion that He may make it prevail over all the religions; and Allah is enough for a witness."[90] (Surah 48:28). The Quran expands the vicegerent to include the Islamic idea of prophethood because the prophets guide humanity toward *true religion*. In the next chapter, we will discuss guidance; when humanity submits to Allah, they empower themselves with contracting authority to self-deliver.

The focus on Will and "guidance" permeates the Islamic narrative by developing a contractual understanding of the world. Their contractarian model forms religious strictures to control society and marriage.

Implications of Diverse Views

How does the creation of Adam in each text demonstrate the various aspects of deity? Yahweh seeks to dwell with and come alongside his creation, creating Adam as an image-bearer of himself. The image of God opens the door to further interactions for a divine-human relationship. The image-bearer stewards care for Yahweh's Creation.

Allah maintains a position of loftiness when he creates Adam without sharing his image but endows him with knowledge and authority. He places him in a position to rule and master the world. The divine knowledge enables the submission mandate to continue without the personal interactions of Allah. Allah has adequately allowed his vicegerent to rule over the creation—including angels.

God's image-bearer and Allah's vicegerent are both honorable titles that link humanity to the purpose of either a covenant or contract model. The image-bearer motif focuses more on relatable characteristics, while vicegerent connects to a position. Both narratives present grand ideas to enable humanity to accomplish the divine will. The granted biblical image of God on Adam also allows the granting of knowledge and authority. However, his knowledge deepens since Adam knows more about the nature and essence of God by the fact that he, as an image-bearer, bestows a greater intimate knowledge of the one he replicates. Yet the Islamic knowledge differs quite a bit, much like understanding the cognitive knowledge of one's boss's desire and intent for a particular work, but not like intimately knowing a close friend's wishes, longings, and intentions—the latter intimate learning grants a richer, far more superior knowledge to form a closer relationship.

Authority exists in both accounts, but the foci differ. Humanity, to dwell with deity and bear his image with earthly dominion, differs from the Islamic Adam. One demonstrates a Creator who communicates through covenant promises, which accepts mutually dwelling with God and each other as spouses. The biblical authority centers on relationship and promises—motivated by unconditional love. The narratives of each text differ since the Bible depicts a relational covenant narrative while the Quran formulates a directive contract. The contractarian model points to a deity who manages by contracted power to establish a place to submit more than a mutual dwelling together. With his sheer control over humanity, Allah does not concern himself with helping or relating to them but forms bowing servants to his power. His authority, based on responsibilities and obligations, motivates the adherents solely by fear and judgment.

Dwell with Yahweh or Submit to Allah?

The discussion centers on whether humanity was made to dwell obediently with Yahweh or submit without a divine-human relationship to Allah. In the Bible, Adam and Eve were responsible for ruling, but the passage's focus highlights their dwelling with or dwelling without Yahweh. On the other hand, the Absolute-Oneness viewpoint stresses knowledge and authority to submit to Allah without any near-dwelling experience. So the question remains: *What is the purpose of humanity in the Bible and the Quran?* The Bible emphasizes that a core purpose enables dwelling with Yahweh, which differs from Allah's established purpose toward submission.

The Old Testament scholar John Walton sums up Creation distinctly, "When God made this cosmos, he made it for a particular reason, he made it to be a place for his dwelling. He didn't need a dwelling but the reason he made it a place to be his dwelling is because he made it for us so that we can dwell with him. You see what God has always wanted is to be in relationship with his people."[91] The human purpose seeks to relate and dwell with God. The purpose of Creation was not just to establish a contract ruling of submission but to dwell with God, promoting a deeper connection to the Creator.

Dwelling with Yahweh later reflects in the New Testament prayer of the Lord Jesus, "I in them and you in me, that they may become perfectly one, so that the world may know that you sent me and loved them even as you loved me" (John 17:23).

Implications to Marriage

The Bible shows a covenant model in which covenant-Yahweh creates a world to dwell with him, based on promise and relationship. The Quran displays a contractarian model into which the contract-Allah places and structures a world to submit to certain religious strictures.

Biblical marriage reflects Yahweh's desire to share and dwell together. As Creator, he bestows his image *in* humanity, inspiring humanity through a covenant to dwell together. Sharing his image and connecting his presence to one's marriage demonstrates covenant unity—joining two persons with God. God dwells with and alongside Adam and Eve, similar to how marriage reflects dwelling with and alongside each other. The husband and wife reflect the male-and-female image replicating lovers who come alongside and desire to dwell with each other. Like their Creator, they pursue loving, providing, and forming connections. Thus, the divine-human relationship parallels a covenant marriage.

Yahweh's unity of persons conveys to the marriage a similar joining of two persons to reflect a marital oneness. The marriage focus establishes more of a *be-and-becoming* relationship than *a submit-and-do* obligation. This focus seeks to identify the basis of the relationship without ignoring the element of human responsibility or obedience. At Creation, Adam and Eve sought to become one flesh and be persons who dwelt with their Creator. Sin marred this hope and introduced tendencies of dysfunction in marriages. Broad brush strokes will form a foundation for future studies in this exposure to what lies below the surface. Granted, in Christian marriage, respectful and sacrificial roles stem from the unity and order sourced in the Creation account. In my future writings, I will study them in more detail. Unfortunately, many writings consumed with marital roles do not see what treasures exist below in how marriage reflects our relationship with our Creator. The covenant blueprint forms a mutual bond in dwelling with each other in oneness more than mutually attempting to obligate each other into certain roles.

This chapter provides a foundation for understanding how humanity relates to their Creator and introduces significant implications relating to marriage. The marriage contract in Islam relates to Adam's position since Allah grants him honor and guidance to live according to Allah's Will. These ideas are also expressed in Islamic marriage when the husband's position of privilege over his wife guides his family in this pre-determined religious structure. The husband's endowed guidance sets up the wife's submission.

Absolute Oneness mandates and requires submission from humanity. As Creator, his detachment defines itself over Adam by placing him as vicegerent to rule. The vicegerency enables Adam to be a deputy with established contractual terms. The union of Allah and Adam join in purpose without any semblance of unity. Any perceived union creates an Islamic sense of submission. The contract-Islamic union mandates communication from above, proper ranking from above, and proper guidance from above. The Islamic marriage joins two in a contract emphasizing interaction according to placement and authority. As a semblance of the *Khalifa*, the husband ranks above and is positioned in control to maintain marital obligations. Islam consistently recalls the husband's divine placement over his wife, so she must submit to her husband's will. A distinct contract identity becomes evident.

Conclusion

This layer of creation will open the discussion of divine deliverance. Deity's distinct natures position Yahweh or Allah to a particular way of working and interacting with the world. One works in relational unity, while the other works alone. Yet, in both systems of thought, the interactions of divinity with humanity are consistent in their inner designs to enhance a covenant or contract perspective.

My fellow Central Asian teacher previously asked, *What kind of question is that? That is such a silly question. Why are you asking this?* However, after a two-hour discussion on the implications of placement, he said *that question, "Who is higher, man or angels?" depicts one of the most critical issues for believers.* The query determines one's view of humanity and, eventually, the workings of salvation. Let's now look at biblical salvation and quranic self-deliverance.

Yahweh's nature regarding Creation	Allah's nature regarding Creation
Dwells in and alongside	Exalted above
Man created in God's image.	Man as vicegerent
Spirit hovers over Creation	Allah is not a Spirit
Focus on relationship	Focus on placement
Be-and-Become mandate	Submit-and-Do Mandate
Programed for Divine Relationship	Programed for Divine Power
Indwelled Followers	Guided Followers

Chapter 4 – Manner of Deliverance

Muslims believe that salvation is a matter of doing more good deeds than bad.

To me, sin was bad, but not that bad. – Nabeel Qureshi[92]

In Nabeel Qureshi's book, *Seeking Allah, Finding Jesus,* the author shares his journey of spiritual searching. His search to find Jesus occurred over a multi-year conversation with his friend David. For many of our Muslim friends and acquaintances, salvation is not just a decision but a multi-staged journey of challenged presuppositions. In exploring the foundations of how deliverance in the Bible and the Quran differ, a believer needs to consider presuppositions about deity, the creation of humanity, and sin. Therefore, this chapter will look at a few aspects related to the self-delivery ideas of Islam in light of biblical salvation.

Interactions stem from one's nature. How does a deity who, by nature, desires to connect, dwell, and come near to save his beloved? How does a lofty deity deliver those to whom he gives guidance? The stories are different—one sends himself, the other his authorized Will. The Bible provides covenant-promised salvation through the divine-human relationship, while the Quran's endowed responsibility encourages the path of self-deliverance. The Bible and the Quran present different manners of deliverance. Christianity presents savior-provided salvation, while Islam presents a form of self-deliverance.

In biblical understanding, the profound idea that all of humanity bears his image opens the door for God to dwell with humanity. God, in His love, does precisely this—he becomes a man. The Lord Jesus, a fully and truly God-man, sacrificially provides a covenant promised salvation.

In contrast, a non-image-bearing deity provides guidance and his will. Islam denies man is made in God's image, so Muslims cannot even imagine how the Word of God can take on flesh (John 1:14). The Bible amplifies covenant salvation, while the other promotes contractual self-deliverance.

Each person desires to hear one's Creator declare deliverance from condemnation and acceptance by him on the day of judgment. However, covenant and contract deliverance presuppose different paths to gain peace, so let's go beneath the surface to find the water of life.

The Water of Life

On a few occasions, I visited the Hagia Sophia in Istanbul. The beautiful former church is a sixth-century architectural miracle and wonder. However, many people do not know as they walk on the streets and courtyards near this wonder that below are cavernous cisterns that supplied the ancient city with water. This city boasts eighty of these archaic water storage facilities, many of which have massive pillars supporting them. A few near the church are open to the public, but outside the south Hagia Sophia courtyard lies an unmarked enclosed area showing an upper cistern covering. The lower levels in the vicinity, hidden from the public eye, form multiple stable cistern pillars that support the massive church structure. Numerous covered openings in the church building lead to these ancient wells or air culverts supporting the building.[93] Archeologists recorded over 900 meters of underground culverts near this location, benefiting the structures above.

Today, many walk on and observe only the surface of society, yet below exists similar hidden chasms. Will they find the lower cistern as a source of water or just a space with dry sand? A thorough search will expose the many pillars which support the external ideas of deliverance. For example, Christianity proclaims Jesus as the resurrected Savior of the world, while Islam calls out daily for all to come and submit to Allah. How does a deity in either a covenant or contractual framework deliver? For this reason, we will dig below the surface to discover how each narrative presents sin, salvation, and sacrifice.

Yahweh's Provision vs. Self-deliverance

Specific words clarify how Yahweh and Allah work. Yahweh, the covenant-pursuing deity, provided salvation to humanity through the sacrifice of Christ. Allah, the contract-pursing deity, enabled deliverance for humankind by the provided guidance placed in the essence of man. The covenant truth shows what I call a "Savior Salvation" that describes the deliverance the Lord Jesus provided for any who will repent of their sins and believe that he is their Lord and Savior.

For Muslims, a contrast becomes necessary since they reject the biblical Savior. The Muslim scholar al-Faruqi, who wrote much about comparative religion, provides a thought-provoking contrast, "Indeed, salvation is an improper term, since, to need 'salvation,' one must be in a predicament beyond the hope of ever escaping it. But men and women are not [in] that predicament. Humans are not ethically powerless. They are not helpless puppets capable of neither good nor evil. They are capable of both. Their pride and glory are to 'save' themselves by deeds and works."[94] For al-Faruqi, the disparity with Christianity provides clarity. He digs below to reveal that in Islam, men and women are capable of saving themselves. Their Islamic foundation, sourced from the desert sands of Arabia, does not show a savior. Their capability, which I call self-deliverance, becomes a point of pride and ability. Allah sets up a pact so humanity, through submission, provides one's self-deliverance. On the other hand, the Bible teaches the lostness of humanity and the need to find the water of life, sourced in Jesus, who came to seek and save the lost (Luke 19:10). Only God's provision of salvation will keep them. These specific terms will convey the presuppositions of deliverance.

Depths of Sinfulness

When we dig and uncover preconceptions, Islam presupposes man to have guidance. In this viewpoint, they overlook any ideas of depravity and the neediness for a savior. But the biblical perspective declares the lostness of humanity:

- "None is righteous, no, not one." Rom. 3:10
- "For all have sinned and fall short of the glory of God." Rom. 3:23
- "For the wages of sin is death." Rom. 6:23
- "Behold, I was brought forth in iniquity, and in sin did my mother conceive me." Ps. 51:5

Every person is born with a sinful nature that separates them from a holy God and places on them a death sentence. First, we experience a physical separation when we die, but sin also separates us spiritually and relationally from God's Spirit. The third phase of death, eternal separation from God, comes because each of us in this life *falls short of the glory of God.* In this paradigm, no room for personal honor or self-delivery becomes possible. One may think this system unjust, but God, as the divine judge, condemns sin and offers the provision of salvation.

The sinful nature inherited from Adam makes all sinners who need a savior to redeem them (Rom. 5:12). The sinless Christ provides salvation, a promise of sin's payment. God's great love is no surprise for Christians since one of his Old Testament names is Yahweh *Yireh,* the provider. "And Abraham called the name of that place *Yahweh will provide,* for which reason it is said today, on the mountain of Yahweh *it shall be provided."* (Gen. 22:14, LEB, emphasis mine). The sacrifice given to Abraham demonstrated more the provision of Yahweh than Abraham's great faith since *all have sinned and fall short of God's glory* (Rom. 3:23). God's love, exemplified in the sacrificial animal provided for Abraham, gives. God's provision shows a great divine sacrifice.

Our neighbor in Central Asia gave birth to a newborn son. When we visited their home to congratulate them, we often found the baby wrapped in tight linens and laid in a wooden crib called the *gavara.* This *gavara* crib enables the parents to bind the child tightly to keep warm and contained in a safe environment. This crib gave us a new way to think about our Savior as a baby wrapped in swaddling clothes. The Central Asian parents initiate their ritual of placing a baby into the *gavara* by whispering the Islamic *Shahada*[95] into the newborn's ears seven times. Like a mantra, this statement is repeated innumerable times during any family or religious ritual. The parents intend for the words to guide the newborn as a means toward Allah and what his messenger promoted. The repeated words initiate guidance, so the little one will begin to obtain the knowledge to keep on the Path.

Much like a contract, the Shahada acts as a witness in committing to Allah's absolute oneness. This initial declaration for Muslims decrees their obligation to a specific path of responsibility and verifies their intended faith.

Sahih Muslim gathered hearsay words of their messenger in his collections of traditions called the *Ahadith.* One of them was, "I created My servants in the right religion, but the devils made them go astray." This fear of going astray encouraged the placement of numerous amulets on the newborn's *gavara* and the practice of repeated Arabic religious sayings to gain protection. For the newborn Muslim, these practices link belief and future practice.

Fitra – Predisposition toward Islam

The verbalized, repeated words coincide with another pre-supposed concept found below the surface, called *fitra*,[96] which means innocence. For Muslims, each person is born in innocence. This Islamic virtue enables one to keep to the way of Islam without being led astray. They believe the *fitra* within each newborn inclines them toward Allah's oneness and contract of submission. A Muslim has guidance *(hidayah)*, which resembles the word *hadiat*, which means gift, enabling each person to submit.[97] In Islamic thinking, humanity is neither lost nor deprived, not needing salvation. They believe all newborns are born Muslims, and their parents or environment make them something else or, as the above tradition references, that the devil made them go astray.

Implications to Depravity and *Fitra*

"Two roads diverged in a yellow wood,
And sorry I could not travel both
And be one traveler, long I stood
And looked down one as far as I could
To where it bent in the undergrowth;"
Robert Frost[98]

As we stand by each path and look down as far as possible, the consequences of each will be apparent. One cannot travel down both approaches in this world, and both ways cannot be correct. Let's look at where the diverse viewpoints travel to determine a manner of deliverance. Depravity requires a divine sacrifice, while *fitra* needs "guidance."

Sacrificial Death

In the biblical creation story, God fashioned man as the image of God, enabling his presence to dwell with humanity. But death reigned over them after humanity sinned in the Garden of Eden. A separation occurred—physically, out of the garden, and spiritually, separated from a relationship with Yahweh. Now, only payment of death could deliver them. The scriptures clearly state that *without the shedding of blood, there is no forgiveness* (Heb. 9:22). The love of God reached down and provided skins for the first couple and a lamb for Abraham. Later, the Son of God was the lamb who died for the sins of the world (John 1:29). A pattern of a sacrificial death depicts God's love reaching down to humanity.

The divine sacrifice counters the depth of sin. The holy sacrifice flows from the heart of God to show how he communicates. He pursues and sacrificially loves the beloved. The Muslim scholar A. B. Philips interestingly defines why Christians believe God became a man:

"This belief required a reason, for which the concept of original sin and divine sacrifice were invented. It was claimed that due to the sin of Adam, which accumulated down the generations until it became so great that no human sacrifice could remove it, a divine sacrifice was needed. Consequently, God had a human son, who was God, Himself, incarnate. God's son later died on a cross as a sacrifice for all humankind to God, Himself. The son, who is God, Himself, was later resurrected and currently sits on the right side of God's throne waiting to judge humankind at the end of this world."[99]

For the Christian, the skepticism of Philips is apparent. But let's clarify: man cannot remove sin, nor were reasons invented for *a divine sacrifice*, but God's love compels him to sacrifice for humanity. *A divine sacrifice* is not possible in the Absolute Oneness rationale because each contract presupposition eliminates the need for it. His skepticism mentions the incarnation, God becoming man, a concept that a lofty Allah finds unacceptable. The reason for this tremendous divine sacrifice of love is the curse of death on Yahweh's beloved image-bearers. However, skeptics ignore the more excellent reason for God's great love. *God so loved the world...*, the supreme motivation for

73

the divine's love forming a God-toward-man relationship that runs counter to a man-toward-God religion.

Humanity tends to rationalize truth when one hears something misaligned with one's perspective. The non-invented gospel found in Christ is the only way to God. The heart of the gospel focuses on two eternal truths denied by Islam: the person of Christ and his sacrificial death. The Islamic submission mandate tears out the heart of the gospel, only to insert the contractual self-deliverance as a means for humanity while simultaneously ignoring the hope of glory, Christ (Col. 1:24)!

Philips defensively mentions incarnation but places the Lord Jesus only as a human son and repeats the word *Himself*, especially in connection to Christ's death, to counter the heart of the gospel, which is that God himself, as the eternal Son and Word, provides the sacrifice. Philips denies the gospel, remaining unconvinced, so he keeps to the motto, "One who is convinced against his will is of the same opinion still." Despite his commendable insights, his desire rationalizes away the great truths of the gospel. He is digging in North America to find ancient Middle Eastern artifacts, only to come up empty. The Islamic contract perspective created many historical layers to support its own premises while at the same time denying the very foundation underneath them—the Word of God in the Old and New Testaments.

Re-defining Sacrifice

The role of sacrifice in Islam is different from that of the Bible. Islamic focus obscures the provision of a loving God since their great

Key terms	Covenant Salvation	Contract Submission
Need a term here?	Savior provided	Self-deliverance
Deity's role	God provides Himself	Allah provided Guidance
View of sin	Total depravity	Forgetfulness
State of humanity	Lost	Guided
Repentance's definition	Change of mind	Change toward Submission
Related terms	Covenant	Contract
Identity	Child of God	Slave of Allah
Ability for Salvation	Powerless to save self	Powerful to save self

faith in their prophet re-focuses their narrative. Islamic thought sees humanity empowered by guidance to self-deliver himself with some aid from Allah to keep on the right path. *Man sacrifices* to submit. For these reasons, the yearly celebration of a man's willingness to sacrifice occurs in the Islamic lunar month of *Dhu al-Hijjah*. Each year, the significant events and rituals act as a collective Islamic identity for each Muslim. Their sources ignore the biblical system in which God provides the sacrifice and sacrificially moves to love the sinner. In Islam, the sacrifice motif re-defines and re-legitimizes the historic contract narrative.

Exiting my apartment in the afternoon on the day of Islamic sacrifice, the evidence of sacrifice appeared before me. First, drops of blood dotted the corridor to demonstrate at least one neighbor's sacrifice that day. Then, there were the signs of blood puddles on the street near the gutter in which a severed cow head remained. All gave evidence of the remembrance of Abraham's act of faith and now a neighborly display of faith. Some neighbors portrayed great faith by killing a sheep or a cow, hoping like Abraham to pass Allah's test. They share the meat with others, especially those in need. This re-defined sacrifice emphasizes individual faith to gain personal benefit. The emphasis leans toward the human effort, not toward a divine sacrifice. A Muslim strives to remain within the terms of a self-deliverance contract through personal initiatives and good works. On the Islamic day of sacrifice, the remembrance of the human self-sacrifice takes center stage while ignoring the provided divine sacrifice.

The website *whyislam.org* says, "Abraham's selfless act of obedience is commemorated by the sacrifice of a domestic animal such as a lamb, sheep, cow, or goat, the meat of which is then distributed to relatives, neighbors, and the poor... Eid-ul-Adha exemplifies the charitable instincts of Muslims in their communal effort to see that no one is left deprived of the sacrificial meat. It further embodies the values of discipline and self-denial and submitting to the will of Allah."[100] The emphasis in this re-defined mode of sacrifice shows a selfless act toward self-denial to enhance one's submission. Forgotten is that God himself provided the ram for

Abraham and the symbolic reference to God's Son sacrificed to fulfill the penalty of sin.

The Scope of Guidance

Much like a contract, the Islamic self-deliverance notion guides those under obligation. Islamic guidance connects to the inner bent called *fitra,* which predisposes the individual to seek the right way. Surah 3:20 states that if one surrenders or submits, then they are rightly guided or on the right path. Surah 20:123 concurs, "He said: Get forth you two therefrom, all (of you), one of you (is) enemy to another. So there will surely come to your guidance from Me, then whoever follows My guidance, he shall not go astray nor be unhappy."[101] The two mentioned in this passage describe Adam and his mate, whom we know as Eve but her name is never mentioned in the quranic text. They have *guidance* and are tasked to follow the guidance given. Commentary on this verse, "God has not abandoned humankind after creating them rather He has always shown the path that leads to Him. *It is then up to the people* if they want to seek and benefit from that guidance or not." (Italic mine).[102] In their thinking, a person relies on actions of deliverance rather than on God's sacrifice to save or provide a savior. Like contract terms, the signees follow, seek, and benefit from the agreed submission contract. Islamic Guidance is often described as the Path—the proper Islamic manner of living- so the onus depends on each person to stay on the Islamic Path.

Notice the repeated terms in Surah 5:16: "Wherewith God *guides* all those who seek His pleasure to the ways of peace, and He brings them out from darkness into the light by *His Will* and *guides them* to the Straight Way (Islamic Monotheism)." Those in *the Straight Way* know Allah's Will and Guidance. In contractual thinking, submission leads to the Path or the Straight Way, as stated in the verse. In his exalted aloneness, this deity sets them up for success without coming alongside them or dwelling with them. His guidance always points back to the Path he has set up.

The terms mentioned could portray intimacy (guide, Will, peace, Way), but they only connect to capacity and duties. In this *Straight Way*, humanity lacks an intimate connection with Allah because they neither bear an image nor allow the indwelling of his presence. The non-personal focus avoids personal interactive relationships but points to a known, unchanged Will to submit to. For this reason, Persian Christians love to say, *We have a relationship with God* without religion. On the other hand, a Muslim will declare they have the *right* religion, which focuses on a set of laws in a community. Much like Robert Frost's wood, the Islamic Path is *bent in the undergrowth* of Islam.

The Right Guidance

One day in Central Asia, I worked in my garden in front of our house. Our street was often busy—shepherds herding their sheep, amateur entrepreneurs selling their wares, neighbors on visits, and children going to or returning from school. My garden was also on the way to the mosque. As I worked in the garden, neighbors often started a discussion with me. One such man, a religiously devout youth in a prayer cap, approached me with a brief message before his jaunt to the mosque: "We have the *true* religion." He awaited my response, challenging me with his intense, downward gaze. Finally, I quipped, "I *know* the true God." While this comment may not have been the best way to share the truth, it highlighted a crucial difference between our respective deities. The God of the Bible, Yahweh, desires and actively seeks to be known, encouraging relationship. My friend's perception of God, on the other hand, promoted a deity who heads an elaborate system of behavior. His attempt to *evangelize* me was an invitation to the *true* religion, a particular path, and conformity to what he thought was true. For him, a submission in a contract was more important than a covenant relationship.

I sincerely believe that a Christian who understands the depth of the gospel and the completeness of salvation in Christ will never turn from this promised eternal life to follow any other religion. The tradeoff is incomprehensible. In Christ, we have the assurance of the forgiveness of sin by God's promises, which *true religion* cannot offer. We are justified in the eyes of God because of His sacrificial death (Rom. 3:24–25). In Christ, the very presence of God in the Holy Spirit indwells us, guaranteeing eternal life with God (Eph. 1:13), which *true religion* neither allows nor can ensure. A former Shia Ashura leader[103] said, "The Word of God grants salvation to us so to be a child of God and heirs with Christ Jesus, but in Islam, there is no value in one's self but to be a servant or slave of Allah." The Holy Spirit and the Word of God sanctify believers to grow in Christ's likeness.[104] The promise of eternal life depicts glorification, where resurrected believers will eternally dwell with God as his people.[105]

Salvation's understory, when understood, becomes quite distinct and precious. For each of us to understand our lostness and overwhelming need for salvation initiates awareness of our Creator's love. Praise be to God for offering himself!

In Central Asia, my Christian world and the Islamic Path diverged to encounter each other. So, this religious youth, in reality, was inviting me to give up the promised assured salvation—the justification of my sins in God's sight, the very presence of God in my life, dwelling with Christ, and the eternal hope of dwelling with God—so that I could endeavor to try and please the Absolute-Oneness deity who refuses to indwell me, never granting assurance and who will not guarantee a future to dwell with him. The choice is obvious for anyone who understands the hope of the gospel. On that day, we both intended well, one traveler in the garden and the other on the street. Yet, like the poet Robert Frost, "And be one traveler, long I stood. And looked down one as far as I could."[106]

This write-up gives me a personal look down the Islamic Path, to see as far as I can. Hopefully, unlike the religious youth, others will look, contemplate, and find the most amazing divine love. The undergrowth of truth bends not toward the right religion but the right relationship with the divine! Many fear the gospel since the path differs from their upbringing and promises abundant life now and for eternity.

Covenant Salvation vs. Contract Self-deliverance

Christians celebrate the Advent of Jesus, and Muslims celebrate the Advent of the Quran. For Muslims, the Quran embodies Allah's Will, but for us the incarnation of Jesus Christ depicts the Eternal Word coming to dwell among us. Let's look at how these things reflect covenant salvation and contract self-deliverance.

A covenant prioritizes divine-human dwelling, while a contract prioritizes service. Paul F. Palmer, a Christian scholar, states a profound insight, "Contract is used of things, of property or of personal belongings. When persons are involved, it is not the person who is hired or contracted for, but his services."[107] A covenant's promised relationship forms togetherness, while a contract expects to render service to another. The biblical focus portrays God's covenant in relationship with his people. He refuses to abandon Adam in the garden (Gen. 2–3), then later dwells with his people in the desert wanderings (Exodus through Deuteronomy), and fills the temple in Jerusalem with his presence (1 Kings 8). His presence and close relationship with the believing community show his highest priority. Thus, for the Eternal Word to incarnate himself and dwell among humanity should be imaginable.

In the contract religion, the priority is service. The Absolute Oneness deity has revealed his Will. This advent of his Will clearly defines the service expected. To create a contractual link to the past, the Will depicted in the Quran re-focuses the view on Islam. The Quran ignores the relational divine presence with Adam, Abraham, Jacob, and David never repeating them in their traditions or stories. Instead, their narrative promotes words of affirmation toward contract service—submission to the religion of these former prophets. The relational God's dwelling with his people appears in the Old Testament as unfolding stories centered on Yahweh dwelling with his people, not just a service package of obligations.

The eternal covenant of salvation joins us with God in an unbroken covenant unity. If salvation was by works, then a contract forms without a covenant. When one does not meet the contract conditions, the bond separates, and the agreement breaks down. Yet the attitude of a covenant pursues reconciliation even when the covenant relationship breaks because a covenant is never based on works. After all, it illustrates a permanent relational unity.

Religion Centered on Self-Deliverance

Contract self-deliverance places the burden on the follower to pay for sins. Submit, pray, repent, and follow the *Sunnah*[108] of the prophet to overcome and cover one's faults. Surely Allah helps and instills

Guidance for obedience (Surah 47:17), but he does not grant a clear assurance of sins being forgiven. Contract self-deliverance describes Islamic Guidance giving humanity the capability to liberate themselves by following the stipulated dictates of Islam. The Islamic self-ability disallows any understanding of lostness or need for a savior since each man or woman can submit to Islam for deliverance. The contract Guidance defines religious duty by obligation, without any assured forgiveness or promises of eternal life. In this way, the contract narrative stays on the surface as a bond of service.

However, the religious environment of self-deliverance often heavily emphasizes Allah's mercy, while a covenant environment emphasizes divine grace. Calling out for mercy or claiming mercy to cover the sin or mistake becomes familiar in the former atmosphere. Therefore, each surah of the Quran, except one, starts with recalling the name of Allah to be Merciful and Compassionate, which states the high priority of mercy for Islam. Correspondingly, Muslim speakers invoke his mercy when they speak, and the typical person repeats the mercy mantra for daily protection and remembrance. For this reason, Islam focuses on invoking the mercy of Allah so that he will not grant what each person deserves.

The focus on mercy allows an emphasis on remembering Allah. The Arabic word for remembrance is *Dhikr*, and Al-Badr of Saudi Arabia said, "Mentioning Allah opens up the heart to a variety of virtues and a number of ways to serve Him."[109] The contract Deity said, *Remember me and I will remember you* (Surah 2:151). The condition motivates the adherents to remember the deity to gain mercy. Sin, defined as forgetfulness, can only be countered and overcome with remembrance. Daily religious remembrance occurs in a few formats. The daily prayers, weekly Friday gatherings, and the yearly month of fasting are all enhanced forms of remembrance. Amazingly, the daily prayers are repetitious, invoking God's mercy as a means of deliverance.

Furthermore, Muslims often repeat the memorized phrases or verses from the Quran. Even the foundational creed, *Shahada*, encourages remembrance since an adherent recites the creed in prayer throughout one's life. Many individuals clutch prayer rosary-like bands of 33 or 99 beads as they remember and repeat the names of

Allah to re-focus their thoughts. In the Middle East, a person will sit in public, on a bus, or waiting in some location, and their lips pronounce words, but no audible sound is heard. Remembrance takes place. Their devotion to remembering is remarkable. One hadith states the difference between a house that remembers Allah and one that doesn't is life and death. To remember is to live; to forget, death.

The manner of deliverance for contract faith obligates remembrance since Allah is near if practiced (Surah 2:186). If forgetfulness becomes the habit of life, then the door of death opens. Therefore, the contract structure emphasizes forms of remembrance to re-direct the heart and mind toward the Path. Repeated phrases that affirm the set Will and religious Path reinforce the daily manner of self-deliverance. Remembrance, not the Spirit of God, dwells in the adherent. In their understanding, self-delivery becomes impossible for them without the daily prayers, the spoken Arabic phrases, and constant re-focus.

A God-centered Deliverance

In some Iranian churches, a new custom occurs when a person accepts the Lord as their savior. Right after a person comes to Christ, a group of believers will form a circle around the new believer to sing this song:

> *A great celebration, we must sing songs for the Lord.*
> *We will praise him with a new song.*
> *Hallelujah, Hallelujah. Hallelujah, Hallelujah, Hallelujah!*

The rejoicing remembers what the Lord has done to redeem all who come to him. The circle of friends sing and clap to rejoice, much like the angels of heaven. At the moment of salvation, the angels of heaven rejoice! So likewise, each of us present also rejoices for the lost is now found and gives the Lord praise for the great, incredible salvation he delivers.

The song acts as a ritual of acceptance, beginning the relationship of the new believer together with the believing community. God loves us unconditionally, and this love guides believers' lives. The new believer de-emphasizes any possible deserved actions in one's life; the spotlight shines on the loving, grace-filled acts of God who provided salvation for them. A grand celebration occurs on earth and in heaven, so *we must sing songs for the Lord.*

The Bible depicts the covenant-keeping God as a lover and his people as the beloved. The lover sings over his people as he rejoices and exalts over them; some even describe the scene as God dancing over his beloved. The prophet, by inspiration, describes the lover:

> *"The LORD your God is **in your midst,***
> *a mighty one who will save;*
> *he will **rejoice over you** with gladness;*
> *he **will quiet you by his love;***
> *he will **exult over you with loud singing**."*
> Zephaniah 3:17 (emphasis mine)

God is love (1 John 4:7–21), and he does not just have love as a concept or seek to be loving, but this verse passage states: God in love, as a divine being, exudes and overflows his love, avoiding the appearance of an abstract deity. He loves the world so much that Christ died on the cross to pay for the world's sins. He sacrificed himself without expecting reciprocal actions (John 3:16). A love without giving distorts the meaning of love. He sacrificially provided salvation to those who received his gift.

The Scriptures often call Yahweh a father (Isaiah 63:16) or husband (Isa. 54:5) to his people. A father or husband demonstrates the divine lover's heart to pursue and seek those he loves. A father protects, and a husband loves. The Lover-God protects and sacrifices for the beloved. In the inspired love poetry of marriage, the connecting refrain is: *My beloved is mine, and I am his* (Song of Solomon 2:16, 6:3). Similarly, wooed by our lover, we belong to him.

Knowing God vs. Knowing His Will

A contract reveals the requirements desired, affirming obligations as the key aspect to relate to while minimizing the required knowledge of the person. A covenant includes obligations, but its central ethos concerns knowing the other in a promised commitment. In Christianity, we talk about knowing God—his person, will, and commands. The prophet Jeremiah underlines this,

But this is the covenant that I will make with the house of Israel after those days," declares Yahweh: "I will put my law in their inward parts and on their hearts I will write it, and I will be to them God, and they themselves will be to me people. And they will no longer teach each one his neighbor, or each one his brother, saying, 'Know Yahweh,' for all of them will know me, from their smallest and up to their greatest," declares Yahweh, "for I will forgive their iniquity and their sin I will no longer remember." (Jeremiah 31:33-34).[110]

To have sins forgiven and to know God becomes the norm for believers. Neither is it odd to say we know God since the covenant's ethos encourages knowing the one who gave the covenant.

Professor F. B. Huey said concerning the new covenant, "The five 'I wills' in the passage, together with references to 'my covenant,' 'my law,' and 'my people,' clearly demonstrate that as in the other major theological covenants, it would be God taking the initiative. Human history since the garden of Eden (Gen. 3:8–10) has been the story of humankind's flight from God and his pursuit of us. The God who speaks in these verses is a pursuing God, who refuses to leave his people alone to follow their own self-destructive paths."[111] Huey acknowledges Yahweh as a pursuing God, the lover to his beloved people. He encourages each of us: *Know Yahweh!*

Knowing Allah

Can one know Allah? A YouTube video called "Get to Know Allah"[112] depicts Allah as the great Creator and compares him with a world that is *meaningless* and *worthless to Allah.* Shaykh Ahmad Ali eloquently expounds that knowing Allah equates to knowing his greatness and loftiness. However, this Shaykh never references intimate knowledge of Allah, nor any form of dwelling with him, but the video centers on the fear for Allah by revering his position.[113] To know Allah parallels recognizing one's place in comparison to his greatness. To know Allah does not relate to a love for the world he created, which Shaykh characterizes as *meaningless* and *worthless.* The focus becomes knowing Allah's position, not his person, and portraying Allah's greatness, short of any sense in knowing any element of divine pursuing grace for us. Contract knowing only perceives Allah's greatness by submitting to his Will.

Another Islamic website mentions two ways to know Allah, by his creation and by studying the Quran.[114] Allah separates himself from his creation. Hence, a study of creation results only in knowing what he has done, not who he is. In studying the Quran, one encounters silence in pursuit of understanding Allah's person but abounds in revealing his Will or commands. Despite using the word *know*, in reality, the meaning is a misnomer since contract knowing offers these limitations.

Knowledge about someone differs from personal accounts of experience with God. Christians know God exists through Creation (Romans 1:18–23; Ps. 19:1–6; 104), and we know him by his Word. Yet practical ways exist to know Yahweh. His Spirit dwells in us, and we experience him day by day. We walk, abide, and dwell with him (John 15:1–17), "since in [his] presence there is fullness of joy" (Ps. 16:11). Our life and eternal life connect to knowing God daily, including inner dwelling and connecting to our spirit (Rom. 8:16). The Lord Jesus prayed, "And this is eternal life, that they know you, the only true God, and Jesus Christ whom you have sent" (John 17:3). Knowing the God of the Bible encompasses more than knowing his will but includes intimate dwelling together through the great salvation he grants.

For the contract religion, the denial of knowing the God who sent Jesus as savior stands out. Philips, who converted to Islam, mixes metaphors, "To believe that a man is God or that a man became God and to worship that man is the greatest sin and the greatest evil that humans can do on this earth. This understanding is most important because it forms the foundation for salvation."[115]

Philips's starting point warps his perspective since he begins with, "A man is God or that a man became God." Christianity never starts with "a man" but with a loving God who took on flesh (John 1:14). His denial affirms another way of salvation, one which excludes all the beauties of God's love. He does not highlight God's great love for us or even an eternal plan nor prophecies that point to the Lord Jesus Christ. Still, Philips categorizes belief in the eternal salvation plan of God as *the greatest sin* and *the greatest evil that humans can do.* Since he crucifies God again by condemning his eternal plan, our prayer resembles the Lord Jesus, "Father, forgive them, for they know not what they do" (Luke 23:34).

Conclusion

In Central Asia, our organization often helped social homes that housed orphans and single-parent children. One such location needed water since they lacked running water in the building but obtained it nearby. As a humanitarian organization, we made inquiries and had the ground checked to see if there was any water below the surface. We placed a handpump for the staff and children to access the source just nine feet below. We also set up a way to store water, along with a hot water system. One can find a life source, hardness, or just a space by searching below.

Covenant salvation reveals a well-spring of life for those who accept Christ's sacrifice and the indwelling of the Holy Spirit. Contract deliverance offers no assurance, only rules, regulations, and obligations. How one defines salvation and how deeply one defines sinfulness in humanity make all the difference. Defining deliverance as a covenant or contract, a personal knowing of God himself, or just knowing a contracted Will determines direction. These paths of deliverance will espouse different ideas concerning sanctification that we will explore in the next chapter. For many, the manner of deliverance may be theoretical. However, exposing ideas about sanctification will further demonstrate how one lives out either a covenant or a contract framework.

Covenant Salvation	Contract Self-Deliverance
Provided by Divine Sacrifice	Provided by Religious Submission
God Pursues	Adherent Pursues
Knowing God	Knowing Guided Will
Prioritizes Relationship with God	Prioritizes Service for Allah
Based on the Advent of Jesus	Based on the Advent of the Quran
God-toward-man Relationship	Man-toward-God Religion

Chapter 5 – Covenant Sanctification and Contract Conformity

Islam is much more than a system of theology; it is a complete civilization. – Muhammad Natsir

As part of my studies on Central Asia, I visited the whirling dervishes in Istanbul. Not knowing what to expect but sensing the spiritual nature of the event, I approached the occasion with prayer and fasting. These Sufis of Turkey whirled and whirled in the center while others chanted to the musical background of a timpani and flute. The intensity of their whirling mesmerized the crowd, not just for two or three minutes but for fourteen minutes. How they could twirl without dizziness, falling, or bumping into each other was beyond me.

They hoped to connect to Allah to bring a blessing down to the people. One hand lifted its palm upward to receive the blessing, and the other faced downward to give benefit to those present. Later, as part of their worship, the whirling dervishes served food to bring benefit from above in the form of food to those present. They desired to be channels of blessings for Allah. Does he have whirling partners who can connect to the adherents below? Even in this setting, social conformity was evident in how they dressed and worshiped. They desired to commune with Allah, claiming a blessing. The Sufis whirled to defend this possibility of knowing that evening while observers witnessed their religious dance.

The Bible highlights an inward dwelling of God's Spirit as the key to sanctification, while the Islamic contract focuses on external conformity. The practice of one's faith takes on various forms. Both settings demonstrate how they live a practical form of their inner beliefs. Understanding the difference between Covenant Sanctification and Contract Conformity will benefit how a believer from the contract context needs to move and grow in the salvation provided by Christ. Contract Conformity describes Islamic compliance whereby each adherent seeks to abide by the proper socio-religious community (*Ummah*) obligations. For believers and ministers, understanding the elements of Contract Conformity will enable us to speak into the lives of those from this background.[116] Unfortunately, simplicity often dominates one's thoughts concerning a subject, i.e., Christians walk by faith, not by law, while Muslims follow the law (*Shariat*). This chapter will go beyond simplicity because both perspectives desire to form a complete social transformation, which relates practically to how a couple lives.

Background to Sanctification and Submission

We have explored the nature of Allah of Islam and God of Christianity. One is an Absolute Oneness without a partner or associate in any way or form. Yet, Oneness in Trinity comes alongside to share his image with humanity. These two distinct deities communicate differently and relate differently in how they create. So how do contract adherents committed to self-deliverance live out their religion? How do the people of faith in God's covenant live out their beliefs? Both take different paths. Two core questions before us: *What is sanctification?* And *how is submission lived out?*

What is Sanctification?

Sanctification is challenging to define. Indwelling or Covenant Sanctification involves a personal indwelling of God's Spirit so that a believer slowly transforms into Christ's likeness. Sanctification does not just reflect an external separateness but focuses on living out a new identity granted by God. The believer dies to himself and gives way to the living Christ within so that every moment yields to the Spirit's direction. After God's declaration of standing righteous in Christ, the believer's inward growth process starts with the indwelling presence of God to conform to his image (Rom. 8:29 and 2 Cor. 3:18) and fulfill the mandate *to love the Lord our God* (Deut. 6:5) with one's whole being.

Sanctification is Indwelling

"Do you not know that you are God's temple and the Spirit of God dwells in you?" (1 Cor. 3:16, LEB).

In a survey of Christians born into Muslim families, I asked what differs between Christianity and Islam. I remember the response of an Iranian man, a believer, who said without hesitation, "Oh, that is easy; it is the Holy Spirit! They do not have the Holy Spirit." The indwelling of the Holy Spirit presents a great gift and privilege for all believers. The Holy Spirit makes intimate communication and dwelling possible as God abides with us.

In contrast to inward dwelling, external rules exist. We can know the law cognitively and often forget the law's relevance. However, overlooking an indwelling for believers in Christ becomes impossible since the Spirit continually bears witness to our spirit that we are his children (Rom. 8:17). The Holy Spirit's constant presence empowers the sanctification process.

The Contract Path has a Guidance principle supposedly within its nature, but the covenant believer has the guidance of a personal divine presence in them. The Holy Spirit is a personal guide. The scholar Susanne Calhoun said, "The Spirit's indwelling (and through the Spirit, the indwelling of the full Godhead) bespeaks the reconciled intimacy that has occurred between God and humanity. The New Testament records the radical shift: God's people no longer need to visit the temple to encounter his *presence* or stand in the sacred realm of the Spirit. Rather, they themselves have become God's holy dwelling place."[117] Covenant sanctification defines an indwelling presence of the Holy Spirit so that *the radical shift* takes place. Sanctification is never marked by a place, a position, or even simply external moral vestiges but a communion with the presence of God on a daily, moment-by-moment basis.

Sanctification is Impartation

Covenant Sanctification, more than just an indwelling of God himself, imparts life to the believers. Paul, by inspiration, said, "I have been crucified with Christ. It is no longer I who live, but Christ who lives in me. And the life I now live in the flesh I live by faith in the Son of God, who loved me and gave himself for me" (Gal. 2:20). Christ living in the believer imparts life. Salvation depicts the simultaneous events consisting of being baptized by the Holy Spirit into the body of Christ along with the Spirit's dwelling. Death-to-life transformation takes place. The believer dies to self, sin, and the observance of the law to be made alive by the Spirit. Along with the Word's spiritual food and the community of believers, this indwelling provides the means for practical sanctification. Oswald Chambers alludes: "When I pray— 'Lord, show me what sanctification means for me,' He will show me. It means being made one with Jesus. Sanctification is not something Jesus Christ puts into me: it is *Himself* in me."[118]

Sanctification is a New Identity

In salvation, the divine indwelling gives birth to a new identity. The Muslim label relates to one's birth family, yet this idea differs from becoming a Christian since believers are not born Christian. A new spiritual birth must take place after one's physical birth. Covenant Sanctification lives out the unique identity of spiritual birth in which the new self becomes alive in Christ (2 Cor. 5:17).

When united with Christ, a new identity forms the basis of our thinking to encourage us to live like him. Identity supersedes just doing specific actions but indicates a state of being—to be like him. The believer identifies and conforms to Christ's image, not external observances. Out of this identity flows one's actions.

The new identity for believers placed in Christ starts at salvation when all believers are baptized with the Holy Spirit, "All these are empowered by one and the same Spirit, who apportions to each one individually as he wills. For just as the body is one and has many members, and all the members of the body, though many, are one body, so it is with Christ. For in one Spirit we were all baptized into one body—Jews or Greeks, slaves or free—and all were made to drink of one Spirit" (1 Cor. 12:11–13). At the point of conversion, the Spirit baptizes the believer to partake and drink nourishment in this life-giving power (1 Cor. 12:12–13; Gal. 3:27; Rom. 6:3).

Baptism by the Spirit and baptism in the Spirit are the same thing since they describe what takes place at the moment of salvation. Justification co-occurs with the Holy Spirit's baptism since the Spirit seals each believer (Eph. 1:13) in anticipation of a future guarantee of glorification. Any life now lived lives for him (Gal. 2:20; 2 Cor 5:15). The divine dwells in each believer, so we never face daily challenges alone. God's guiding presence empowers us to overcome the power of sin and selfishness potentially.

In Christ, the idea of first-class Christians and second-class Christians does not exist so that no one group is more blessed in status before God than another. On the contrary, the Holy Spirit unites all believers together and unites us with God. Obedience and conformity to God and his word will bring other blessings and benefits, but the status of salvation unites rather than divides. The fruit or lack of fruit may distinguish believers as produce in a market varies by quality. Yet, we all drink and find our nourishment from the same source.

Sanctification Basis on a Church Community

The Word of God challenges the body of Christ to love, encourage, exhort, accept, and submit to one another. Christ as the source nourishes his body. Life in this world challenges every community in how they interact. Yet, a few factors need highlighting for those in the Body of Christ. First, each believer belongs in the body as an accepted child of God (John 1:12). Second, the Spirit of God, who indwells each believer, also cares for and ministers to the body. Third, the Lord Jesus promised his followers an abundant life in the here and now (John 10:10). No community is perfect, but the body of Christ has the spiritual ability to face the challenges that come along.

The sanctification process stands on belonging to the body of Christ. When new believers come into the fellowship, they need to feel they belong to God and other believers; often, this need becomes the foundational cause of growth. For this reason, a church needs to consistently strive to fulfill God's mandate in how they interact.

What is the purpose of this body of Christ, locally? Each church purposes to worship and give glory to the triune God worthy of praise. Worship for the church resembles an act of celebrating what God has done for us. The relational purpose also involves equipping the body of Christ for ministry to each other and into the world. Teaching and preaching present more knowledge concerning God's person and how he works, equipping believers for the work of ministry (Eph. 4:11–16).

The third purpose of the church is to fellowship together. A repeated church saying quips that fellowship consists of a group of fellows in the same ship. The root meaning of fellowship displays a spiritual bond with God the Father and with other believers to represent Christ in this world (1 John 1:3–6). In Christ, all believers unite into the universal church, his body. Their bond of commitment enables fellowship and spiritual interactions together locally and, at times, globally. The divine connection for believers opens the door for a common purpose in relating.

The fourth aim of the church is to evangelize the lost. The Scripture highlights the church's witness to the world, in which the two ordinances of the church, baptism and the Lord's Supper, display their testimony. Believers' baptism publicly demonstrates Christ's death, burial, and resurrection in the new believer's life. The Last Supper illuminates the New Covenant as symbolic of Christ's body broken and his blood sacrificed for our sins. These four purposes are unique and counter the ideas of Contract Conformity.

The acronym WIFE summarizes the church's purposes as the bride of Christ: Worship, Instruction, Fellowship, and Evangelism. Every church should seek to balance these four areas in its community ministry. Unfortunately, many churches emphasize one of these elements over another. Only by the fullness of each of these will a church reflect the WIFE of Christ as his body.

The church community becomes vital to the growth of each believer, especially for those who come from a community-based society. When a church community focuses on political or social ideas, their ideologies often complicate the entry of new persons into the community. Leaders must take care of their church to remain faithful to their primary purposes and not become consumed by the latest talking point.

Believers from an Islamic context struggle with a sense of community when they become a part of a church. When fulfilling its biblical purposes, the church counters the ideas of Islamic conformity.

The church within a non-Christian society often struggles with long-standing prejudices against the majority. However, I have noticed that Persian churches are willing to mix in new believers since most are first-generation believers, often including the new believers in worship and evangelism as they grow in their new faith. Belonging in the new community encourages growth for the new believer and the church.

In the West, *community* entails a sense of individuality, a blind spot for the church. However, the Scripture commands believers to accept, love, and submit to one another, forming inter-connectedness with other believers. In the West, non-connectedness dominates social relationships, while in the Middle East, social connectedness demands conformity. For the Believer from a Muslim background, the church becomes his family. Believers need a Spirit-led balance to pray for wisdom on how to love one's neighbor and other believers best. The church is the body of Christ, devoted to honoring the Lord by loving each other as a spiritual family.

Contract Conformity

Contract Conformity describes Islamic compliance whereby each adherent seeks to abide by the proper socio-religious community (*Ummah*) obligations. Covenant Sanctification, however, depicts an inner relationship with God in which each devotee aims to comply with the internal leading of the Holy Spirit, reflecting more of Christ each day. These two ideals form distinct communities and motivations for living daily.

Suppose one sees sanctification only as a setting apart for God's purpose. In that case, this general definition could cover the religious definition placed even on the Quran—setting one to do God's will. However, they differ in definition and emphasis, which leads to different objectives.

How is Islamic submission lived out? The Path, defined as the correct Islamic manner of living and submission to Allah, offers a form of self-upgrading. Al-Mo'taz clarifies, "The human being can realize righteousness and piety through self-upgrading and seeking Allah's help and support, otherwise one will degrade himself to the lowest class of darkness and misguidance."[119] On the self-upgrading path, we find key ideas such as Guidance, *Sunnah*, *Shariat*, and *Ummah*. Allah's Will, enabled by Guidance, presents three prescriptive ideas that will *help and support* one who follows Islam: *Sunnah, Shariat, and Ummah.* These ideas will be defined in the following paragraphs. The motive in Islamic procedures comes from the duty to conform to the contract religion. In their thinking, the Guidance enables Muslim goodness and the development of an

Islamic society. The writer Umm Zakiyyah summarizes this intent, "We do not stand before Allah because we are already pure. We stand before Allah because we hope to be purified."[120] The individual hope to self-upgrade for purity tends to motivate each person who follows this Path.

Necessary Environment

In Muslim beliefs, all newborns are born Muslims, but their parents and environment make them something else. Therefore, an Islamic climate or society best maintains the Islamic contract-guided path, encouraging an environment for conformity. If the situation can continue, then maintaining submission will result. Contract *sanctification, accurately described as conformity,* is societal because the environment will strengthen the possibility of compliance. The more a society follows Islam, the more Muslims can comply and submit to what they call the *Right Path.*

Muhammad Asad, a Jewish-born convert to Islam, highlights the necessity of an Islamic social contract, "Man does not live in a vacuum. In order that he should be able to grow spiritually and to make the best use of his innate potentialities, he must be protected and assisted by his fellow men. Thus, the inter-relations between the members of the society—and the outward shape of the society as such—have a direct bearing on the spiritual development of every individual with it. The need for social legislation is therefore an unavoidable concomitant of the spiritual righteousness demanded of man."[121]

In other words, inter-relationships in society—and the outward conformity as such—have a direct bearing on the religious development of every Muslim. For them, society needs an outwardly shaped Islamic structure. This *direct bearing* influences the ability for one to develop in submission. Maududi waxes eloquently that, in Islam, "We find such comprehensive moral guidance as can ensure our progress to the highest pinnacle in every sphere of human life and activity. Islam gives us basic moral norms and values to guide and control the entire gamut of man's life. It gives a comprehensive code of behavior for the individual and shows him the way to the highest possible moral excellence and also gives ethical principles on which the edifice of a truly righteous society can be raised and which, if accepted as the basis of individual and collective conduct, can save human life from the chaos and anarchy that have overtaken it today."[122]

The Islamic goal is to form a righteous society so the Islamic community can determine the conduct. The self-upgrading path, a comprehensive code of behavior, reflects a system marked by external implementations, possibly avoiding internal transformation. For these reasons, many Islamic societies are prone to external moral codes with a legal framework. The focus in a contract community spotlights outward conduct.

Sunnah, not Spirit

Keywords in Contract Conformity

Sunnah – The actions and sayings of Mohammad.

Guidance – The innate nature of Islam within man.

Shariat – The Islamic code and rules summarized from the Quran, *Ahadith* and jurisprudent consensus.

The Path – the proper Islamic manner of living.

Ummah – The Muslim community following the Islamic Path.

The Arabic word *Sunnah* refers to the Islamic-approved sayings and actions of their prophet as an example to complement the Quran. According to the Oxford Islamic Studies Online, the *Sunnah* is "inspired by God to act wisely and according to his will."[123] This model centers their contract conformity and replaces any previous examples that may be found in the Bible. The purpose of the *Sunnah* is to reform humanity, enabling the betterment of society with a religious-promoted order.[124] They believe their prophet lived entirely according to Allah's will, and his example marks the model to follow. His life epitomizes Contract Conformity, which rids any notion of the need for a resurrected savior or indwelling Holy Spirit.

Meanwhile, the contract story expects an incarnate evident action to define the contractual Will. For Islam, this Will evidences itself in the *Sunnah*, depicting the actions and words of their prophet. This embodiment of Islam establishes a practical Contract Conformity. The *Sunnah* contrasts with the indwelling of the Spirit of God. So, indwelling, divine sharing, and birthing a new identity misaligned with Contract Conformity. Despite this, Muslims believe that conformity becomes possible when the environment and the external structure reflect Islam.

A specific source of the *Sunnah* comes from the *Ahadith*, which Muslims highly prize and follow for matters not mentioned in the Quran. The *Ahadith* is the plural of *Hadith*, which often is the English rendition of these collections. *Hadith* defines one traditional saying, while *Ahadith* means a collection of hearsay traditions. *Ahadith* means "Report of the words and deeds of Muhammad and other early Muslims; considered an authoritative source of revelation, second only to the *Quran* (sometimes referred to as sayings of the Prophet)."[125] *Ahadith* defines the collection of transmitted hearsay statements of or about Mohammad. The most authentic collections are by al-Bukhara and Sahih Muslim, who compiled the sayings about 215 years after the death of Mohammad.[126] These traditions embodied how to live out the required submission to Allah. In practice, both are highly respected and quoted.

Muslims believe the *Ahadith* as an authoritative source of revelation aligns with the Quran. They say that the Quran is recited and the *Ahadith* is unrecited, which means their book becomes a dictated revelation. In contrast, the other is not recited but hearsay.[127] Islam never classifies these traditions as hearsay, but Islamic law from the Hanafi jurisprudence states, "Witnesses must personally have seen the thing with regard to which they give evidence and must testify accordingly. The giving of hearsay evidence that is to say, evidence of what the witness has heard other people say, is inadmissible . . . But if a witness states that he has heard from a reliable source that a certain place has been dedicated to pious purposes, or that a certain person is dead, that is to say, if he gives evidence of such fact because he heard it from a reliable source, such evidence is accepted."[128]

In most courts of law, hearsay evidence is inadmissible. The *Ahadith* categorize what a person heard from another person that their messenger said or did. Islam identifies those who listened to these things as reliable sources and then consider the statements authentic despite the lapse of over 200 years. Thus, for them, hearsay traditions become acceptable.

The use of these traditions in jurisprudence and practical application becomes quite extensive. The *Ahadith* demonstrates a possible embodiment of a system that portrays a deity who does not share or participate in an incarnate manner. The formative years after the death of their prophet created a body of traditions that articulated the Path and *Sunnah* of Contract Conformity. The creation of the *Ahadith* helped form a new identity based on Islamic thinking, enabling avoidance of the biblical context. Total disinheritance of the biblical past is like destroying ancient artifacts or images. The new traditions invited a way to oppose the biblical emphasis and created a means to defend an Islamic identity.

In a previous chapter, we discussed how believers partaking of God's nature or the Muslims as spectators of Allah's nature formed two paths. The Path of following Allah's Will avoids any personal divine connection. The manner of revelation and deliverance proves this lack of involvement for the receiver. However, in Contract Conformity, a personal physical path displays their messenger modeling the day-by-day Islamic obligations to submission. The *Sunnah* solves the leading solution to a detached deity since the messenger connects personally. The self-deliverance contract reflects the actions and sayings of Mohammad, therefore filling this void of an impersonal deity. The contract narrative needs to move out of the spectator mode to be practical. These practical sayings and deeds are an elaboration and explanation of what the Quran says. In their perspective, Contract Conformity adheres to the right Religion and Path, granting full participation in the Islamic plan.

Guidance Path

The innate Islamic Guidance within each person enables them to live as Muslims. The actions and words of the prophet, the *Sunnah*, *expect* learning and observance. The Path, the manner of correct Islamic living, encompasses an external way of conformity. The writer and former NASA engineer Abdul Hye said, "Islam is a complete Code of Life."[129] Concurrent is Surah 24:54, "Ye shall be on right guidance." The Muslim idea, *fitra* or inner guidance, endows each person so that no new identity will form nor necessitate a conversion—the conforming path pressures submission to the Islamic requirements.

Yusuf Ali states the Messenger's "mission is to train your will and explain clearly all the implications of your conduct. The responsibility for your conduct rests entirely on yourselves."[130] Again, this commentator places the responsibility of self-upgrading on the shoulders of the adherent. The Guidance, Path, and *Sunnah* are known, but the enablement rests with the person despite one's limitations.

Legal System – *Shariat*

The judicial formation of Guidance, *Sunnah,* and Ahadith lead to the Islamic *Shariat.* These items create a tendency for Islam to become more than a religious community but a religious state. The *concepts of Khalifa, ummah, and sunnah* promote a religious state. I do not have space to pursue this line of thinking but only to highlight the total code of community conduct for Islamic life. *Shariat,* or the Islamic law, encompasses the Quran, Sunnah, and the summary of jurisprudent consensus to promote an Islamic social outward conformity for all Muslims. The *Shariat* guides the adherent to live a Muslim life.

In Central Asia, for some time each Saturday, a group of youth came to our house for discussion and dinner. One week, the dialogue took place on what religious law, Shariat, is and the number of religious laws that exist for one to follow. A few of the youth displayed a heavyweight on their faces. Then, a young man named Saeed used his hands to show a long, extensive list of obligations placed on his shoulder. Saeed was miming the burden of Shariat's expectations. The *Shariat* obliges expectations to fulfill the Islamic contract. Yahweh and Allah expect obedience, but the contracted religion expects submission endlessly. Regarding deliverance, the covenant motif places laws as a standard to make one aware of the need for salvation, while the contract bases self-deliverance on behavior. That Saturday, Saeed's charades encouraged sharing the biblical purpose of the law and one's need for a savior.

The scope of the *ummah* reflects groupthink since the desire for societal and community harmony often influences decisions. The *ummah,* by words and actions, pressures conformity to the Islamic

Path in the lives of each community member. The continued external focus contrasts with the covenantal indwelling model.

The Enablement

In Islamic self-upgrading to follow the path of submission, two things empower the adherents; first, the Shariat guides one on how to live the Muslim life. Then, the *Ummah* encourages compliance with Islam. Followers can obtain religious success under the direction of the Shariat and the Ummah.

In commenting on Surah 3:85 and the words, "If anyone desires a religion other than Islam (submission to God), Never will it be accepted of him," A. Yusuf Ali said, "In essence it [religion] amounts to a consciousness of the Will and Plan of God and a joyful submission to that Will and Plan. If anyone wants a religion other than that, he is false to his own nature, as he is false to God's Will and Plan."[131]

Notice the emphasis on religion and the Will. Linking the code of conduct to align with one's nature is a common Islamic argument to validate the logic of how they promote conformity. However, many Christian believers from this background found later that, in Christ, fulfillment was not seeking another *religion* or a code linking to their *own nature* but an internal divine relationship to quench their spiritual thirst. For example, a new believer from Ahvaz, Iran, said, "From Islam's perspective, you need to try by your own strength and by the way of the *Shariat* to become sanctified. But in Christianity, the source is the Spirit, in which we find new birth. He helps us to become sanctified to live like Christ."[132] The Spirit's indwelling initiates divine enablement without the potential for self-enablement.

Islamic Community (Ummah)

Ummah describes the Muslim community following Allah's Guidance. The prime motivator to conform society toward Islam comes from the *Ummah*. Ghulam Haider Aasi, a professor of Islamic Studies said, "*Umma* denotes a community that is based upon a revealed religious and moral norm, but at the same time constitutes a socio-political entity."[133] The *revealed* norm is the Islamic standard, which often desires more than a social identity but even a political one. Many Muslim scholars attest to the ability of the *Ummah* to formulate a religious cohesiveness more than a social influence. Even with the community's overarching impact, the individual ability to sanctify oneself toward Islam results.

In the daily life in Central Asia, we sensed close community living. Every action and behavior seemed scrutinized by our neighbors. What did you bring home from the bazaar? Who entered your apartment as a guest? Did you have a housewarming party when you moved there? If one followed an unconventional way, then questions followed. Each action or lack of response weighed in the neighbors' minds on the neighborhood scale of conformity. I recall a neighbor lady stating her opinion about a minor activity concerning baking bread: *Oh, that's unacceptable.* Such a little action drew attention to the extent of social conformity. The conformity-bent community gives each action moral judgment and often makes them known to those who infringe. How one treats and bakes bread became a moral evaluation for this woman. The perceived weight of responsibility to conform in this environment alludes to the role of the *Ummah.*

The amazing thing about self-deliverance and community conformity is how these two areas bind together. The Muslim faith ties the two closely in an indispensable way. One cannot just leave the faith without leaving the community, nor can one join the community without submitting to the Islamic Path. Despite many external religious attempts to connect to God, like the dervishes of Mavlana, those living in this type of community will know the mandate for community conformity.

Social Conformity

Contrasting Covenant Sanctification and Contract Conformity need further study, and our exploration of key differences only scratches the surface. A more in-depth investigation of the Islamic community requires research to understand better how the community influences those who leave or choose to follow a different faith.

In the daily actions of those who pray five times a day, the Arabic prayers, the words Guide us in the straight Path repeated thirty-two times in one day.[134] The definition of Contract Conformity encompasses reciting, repeating, and remembering to keep on this Path. Outward conformity focuses on compliance with community activities. These replicated mental exercises align with self-deliverance because the responsibility remains on the shoulders of the individual.

During the 1990s, my travel took me to the graves of famous Sufis Mavlana and Naqshbandi. These mystics created the foundation for Sufism, which developed a form of Islamic worship that focuses on introspection and spiritual closeness. On the surface, Sufism desires much of what Christianity offers—an indwelling presence and closeness to God. When visiting Naqshbandi's complex in Uzbekistan, the location was quite simple. The elements of Soviet social conformity marked the simplicity of the area near Bukhara because their religious practices faced Soviet suppression. Despite the communist conformity, they still attempted to follow some of their Sufi practices. For believers, the external pressures to conform to their former community are real, but the political or religious pressure to outwardly conform cannot touch the inner workings of the Spirit. The Spirit of God works on a thoroughly different plane.

In Konya, Turkey the burial site of Mevlana presented a paradox with quite extravagantly decorated Persian writing in a Turkish context. This ancient city, called Iconium during biblical times, has always held a special place in my life. In Acts 14, the social pressure against the gospel existed since Paul and Barnabas preached there. The city became divided with substantial social conformity against them, so they had to flee (Acts 14:4). They fled to a neighboring area. Still, the pressure followed them their new location at Lystra because the "Jews came from Antioch and Iconium, and having persuaded the crowds, they stoned Paul and dragged him out of the city, supposing that he was dead" (Acts 14:19). Despite the social attempt of intimidation, two verses later state, "When they had preached the gospel to that city (Derbe) and had made many disciples, they returned to Lystra and to Iconium and to Antioch, strengthening the souls of the disciples, encouraging them to continue in the faith, and saying that through many tribulations we must enter the kingdom of God" (Acts 14:21–2). Christianity was more than social conformity and still flourished despite social pressure.

During the day, I explored this city, which historically emphasized religious conformity. My exploration took me to the mausoleum of Mevlana, which is dedicated to his remembrance and a form of religious conformity. Despite all the poems about love, which are loosely translated into English, his main work was the poem about the Quran. This work called *Masnavi* is known as the Persian Quran.[135] The focus attempted to lead Sufis toward Allah's kindness, but this still meant conforming to the Muslim Path without any individual freedom for uniqueness. During my last year in Central Asia, I bought this massive work and felt quite happy to see his writings in my Central Asian language. However, the central focus on Islam stood out when I dove into the text. My assessment of the English translations leaned toward much freedom since they favor an individual perspective over the conformity required.

While in the city of Mevlana's death and at his mausoleum, one Iranian tourist commented that all the writing was in Farsi and felt some ethnic pride in the ability to read the ornate calligraphy. Yet in the evening, I met with another group of Iranians in a house church. First, I taught the children an introductory lesson about Christ and then led the main gathering in the Lord's Supper. The occasion was my first time in either English or Farsi to lead a group of believers in communion. The society around us practiced religious conformity much like Mevlana, but in this tiny apartment, the inward communion of the Spirit of God was the focus. Together, we remembered the sacrificial death of our Lord Jesus and worshiped him. As believers from different backgrounds and languages, we still abided with our Savior and the Spirit who dwells in us. We did not need to whirl, conform, or align to a public religious form. That evening, despite being a minority in society, we still worshipped, reflecting the difference between Indwelling Sanctification and Contract Conformity.

For all believers, sanctification initiates inwardly. The indwelling presence of God directs and guides the believer. Faith rooted in Christ produces actions by the Spirit's prompting. The definition of Covenant Sanctification portrays a dying to self, dwelling in the Spirit, and desiring intimacy with God. Sanctification reflects a relationship. Yes, we are set apart for God, but more so, our set place abides in relationship with God who indwells and desires to live through us.

A consistent embedded theme forms: Oneness in Trinity desires to connect and relate to the world through covenant indwelling. God's promises frame our salvation and sanctification, welcoming us into his spiritual family. Continually, God himself indwells the believers and abides with them. Believers are not just living *for God* but living *with him*. The inner spiritual world guides a believer in this world to live and abide with God as one lives out God's will. The covenant-embedded foundation radiates outward in a practical manner.

Conclusion

As evidenced, Covenant Sanctification comes from the indwelling of the Spirit of God, but Contract Conformity forms when one dwells within the standards of the Islamic community. The Islamic social factor enforces compliance with the proper collective identity on the Path, not focusing on heart change, inward diving indwelling or individual rights.

The covenant idea of closeness and relatability through indwelling underpins the why of biblical covenant marriage. Mutual dwelling together in oneness centers the covenant order. Dwelling together furthers their desire to connect and abide when the couple allows the Spirit to indwell their relationship and initiate divine enablement to overcome selfishness.

When new life characterizes covenant marriage, each will pursue one's spouse sacrificially and selflessly. The sacrificial motivation comes more from internal promptings than obligatory external forces. The Holy Spirit dwells in and encourages each believer to abide in Christ, enabling a growth process and requiring each believer to learn obedience and Christlikeness. Christ models covenantal characteristics since he loved till the end and sacrificed himself. Greater love has no man than this to give his life for his friends. Similarly, greater love has no spouse than this: commit every moment to place one's spouse first. Sanctification empowers married couples to reflect the one who sanctioned their covenant to each other by constantly abiding in God's love to grow in Christ's likeness.

Covenant Sanctification	Contract Conformity
Holy Spirit Indwelling	Dwell in conformity to *Ummah*
United with Christ	Hold to the Path
Inward Identity	Outward Identity
Empowered by Spirit	Empowered by Compliance
Fellowship in Christ Unites	*Ummah* Unites
Prayer: Connecting Hearts (God and Believer)	Prayer: Conforming Conduct
Remembrance to Cultivate Relationship	Remembrance to Counter Forgetfulness

While probing how an Absolute Oneness deity functions, a contractarian model appears that structures external codes of religious service, personal sacrifice, and earned social belonging. An external religious world guides each adherent to produce greater conformity. The contract motif entrenches and guards every action, seeking conformity toward Islamic behavior. The Islamic immovable positioning of humanity in connection with his Creator extends into marriage, which becomes a service contract in a community of conformity.

The concluding chapter will consider how these two distinct models produce a different basis for marriage. Covenant marriage mirrors the covenant relationship of Yahweh, while the Islamic contract marriage absorbs the foundational elements of the Muslim faith.

Chapter 6 – What Does Marriage Reflect?

Covenant marriage reflects Yahweh's unity and his covenant with believers, while contract marriage reflects Islamic conformity. Covenant marriage patterns how Yahweh relates when each spouse shares sacrificially, which mirrors the character of the biblical God. The relationship within the divine Godhead loves and forms inner unity.

Many Layers of Marriage

In Central Asia, Islamic *Mazars* saturate the landscape. These graveyards indicate spheres of influence of former, respected religious men. Along with the central tomb are other grave monuments, gardens, and places to gather at these centers. Near to where we lived previously was a major religious site. The main golden-dome ancient building, which the Shia government of Iran renovated, stood in the center of the area. The geometric artwork on the portico entry provided a place to pray for personal deliverance. Elaborate arabesque woodwork structures dotted the courtyard. The Islamic saint buried there was from Iran but is now buried in a dominant Sunni area. How an Iranian-born religious leader who centered his activities in Kashmir ended up in this city in Central Asia is a story of realigning the historic religious focus in the region.

The site was also a burial ground, and as one walked among some of the trees on the east side of the main *Mazar*, evidence of unmarked graves existed. Later, I read that many graves were dug up and re-buried around the sight when they built the main Mazar. A memorial stone was placed on the west side of the building to commemorate this section. However, one of the buildings in the area where my son and I were walking had an open gated door. We entered this small building and descended some steps well below the surface.

Below, we saw an ancient earthen kiln with a three to four-meter radius. My son and I walked around the kiln on a slightly elevated wooden platform. The site was exposed, so one could even touch or enter the ancient furnace, but we took care not to disturb it. A few holes formed on the outer top, most likely to release the heat of the old oven. The site puzzled me. Why was this archaic oven about six meters below the surface, and why was it exposed to intruders like us? At first, I thought the oven must have some historic use with the above *Mazar*.

My neighbor, a history professor at the university, provided the answer to one of my questions. The present city was built on an ancient disastrous landslide, which took place about 1500 years before. The city's northern perimeter displayed a steep hill that edged the town for a few kilometers. These cliffs defined where the mudslide ended when the southern mountain areas slid over the ancient city, and today, this plateaued city sits upon the mudslide tha buried the ancient city. So, the religious compound we stood on was built on top of a portion of the buried city and, by chance, above an ancient kiln. An archaeological dig discovered the kiln, and the building was recently placed over the site to protect it.

Once archeologists realized there was an ancient city below this historic mudslide, they started to excavate and dig trenches, attempting to discover more. The primary discovery besides pottery pieces was the archaic furnace. Despite being below the surface, this evidence gave insight into the town's history. Interestingly, the mudslide enabled the town to build over what existed before. Marriage is remarkably similar. How we see and define marriage today has multiple layers of history. The initial foundations in the biblical and quranic narratives form two marriage models. The insights give focus to what we see around us in our communities — especially in marriage.

This chapter summarizes key foundational differences between biblical and Islamic marriages. The ideas in *Searching Below the Surface* such as the nature of deity, the manner of communication and creation, and deliverance and daily working of adherents, show us patterns and designs that undergird a marriage perspective. These proofs give hints to how we define marriage today.

To address the family issues critically, the scope and beliefs of marriage will be compared and evaluated as two distinct marital systems in the monotheistic faiths of Islam and Christianity. Not all points of view are equally valid, yet both systems have presuppositions that dictate specific marital roles and guidelines. The desired effect clarifies understanding, avoids prejudice, and gleans accurate conceptions to replace common misconceptions. The critical elements of these marital patterns are explained briefly here but fleshed out more thoroughly in the next book, *Defining Marriage: Sketching a Difference Between Covenant and Contract.*

Covenant Marriage is a Unity of Persons
"Bound by the strong cords of God's Love, I ... take you, my bride as my wife, to love and to cherish."

When my wife and I were engaged, we desired to write our marriage vows and memorize them to repeat them verbally on our wedding day. The pastor was prepared to help with the process, but I recall my deep nervousness that day. So, I started, "Bound by the strong bonds of God's love, I..." at that moment, I forgot my name. The severe intensity of the moment or the fact that most of us never say one's name following the pronoun "I." Yet, after a moment of hesitation, I remembered my name and continued from memory to quote our handcrafted vows.

For our marriage, the vows represented the individualized touch of our unity. Marriage joins two persons. Marriage is neither just the joining of two bodies nor an affirmation of similar purposes or situations nor just an economic transaction. Male and female persons join together, witnessed by the Lord to promise in covenant to be one in marital unity.

In chapter one, we identified Yahweh as Oneness in Unity since Father, Son, and Spirit are united, divine persons. The divine unity of persons in the Trinity displays oneness, much like covenant marriage that joins a male and female into a marriage unity. The joining together in marriage reflects more than a union of purpose but an *inward* unity of persons. The idea of a secular union often portrays *external* factors that unify two or more persons to a common cause; for this reason, I prefer the word *unity* to counter this understanding. Similarly, the Trinity is not an external union but a unity of divine persons. Covenant marriage likewise forms a unity of oneness.

When two people make a covenant with each other, they no longer seek an individual approach in life. Marriage, for me, cut into my selfishness. I could no longer explore a selfish bent without bumping into my wife's feelings, concerns, or desires. Everything I now do needs to go through this joined unity. If not, then disunity formed. For us, marriage touched the essence of who we are. If we only made an external decision to join in purpose, then our inner self could not be protected. But marriage unity affects the inner kernel of who we each are.

Covenant Marriage is Oneness

As explored, the oneness in the Bible is a unity of persons. The persons in the Trinity are one all the time, divine in every situation, yet never in disunity at any point nor resembling absolute oneness. In a covenant marriage, the husband and wife become one, which means more than physical oneness but a mystical, spiritual unity that reflects the Trinity of Oneness! This exclusive relationship of oneness spotlights the essence of the marriage but also the basis of one flesh. The one-flesh concept is something they seek to become when they relate together. The becoming one-flesh idea refers to this oneness, but the leaving, cleaving, becoming, and without shame elements of Genesis 2 portray marriage overall. All these ideas incorporate oneness in marriage, the two people in this sacred relationship who leave, become united, cleave permanently together, and share intimately without shame. The essence of marriage reflects moving continually toward oneness together despite the challenges.

Choosing to live in oneness or twoness in our marriage often depends on how we view our needs. Sure, I can look to my own needs and seek to meet them, ignore my wife's needs, and move forward without considering her. These actions promote twoness. Marriage should not be two individuals living their lives independently of each other. Twoness in the marriage relationship exists where each mate exists independently of the other yet retains some connection. A separateness defines the relational connection more than any unity. Twoness in marriage occurs when two persons exist independently in finances, decisions, and marital positions, which seek separateness. Often, twoness results when one spouse gives no concern or thought to one's mate when considering personal desires or needs. But when one consistently considers the other, they promote oneness. Oneness seeks to decide together to honor one's spouse more than any position. Covenant marriage always realizes the bent toward considering the other to form oneness since unity touches every aspect of the marriage.

Covenant Marriage is Relational

Yahweh's unity of persons mirrors the marital unity of persons. He relates within himself as persons, and this divine unity displays self-relatability in the statement that God is love since the eternal persons of the Godhead love. God's love always pursues the beloved. Likewise, in a covenant marriage, each spouse pursues a more significant relationship with the other. Not just connecting physically but seeking mutual greater relational and emotional intimacy. As seen in the Trinity, God relates and connects in his relatable oneness. He is neither self-absorbed nor self-centered in a protective way. A spouse who ignores oneness or marital unity tends toward self-preoccupation. The divine relatability encourages a covenant marriage as more in tune with the "us" of marriage than the "I" or "you."

The relationship between the divine persons is evident since the word of God states *God is love* (I John 4:8). Therefore, love first takes place in and between the divine persons. In this divine love interaction, a perfect unity of oneness creates a world as their object of love. Divine interaction is evidenced in the Creation account when God enters into the first couple's shame, providing communication and a covering for their sin. Similarly, each covenant marriage is bound by the strong cords of God's love to sustain a relationship that considers the other's needs, desires, and expectations. God is still ready to minister and share his love despite the shame and brokenness that naturally result in marriage. Likewise, in moments of marital disgrace, each spouse adopts the divine manner to seek to walk with one's spouse in covering one's shame.

By inspiration of the Spirit, the apostle Paul depicted the love of a husband as reflecting Christ's sacrificial love for the church (Eph. 5:25–32). This love, sourced in the love of God, guides the husband's similar actions. These verses demonstrate that marriage reflects our relationship with God. God loves the beloved unconditionally, and the husband must pursue his beloved wife unconditionally. Again, the couple shares the responsibility to love and submit one to another—tasks that all believers expect to follow.

In a covenant marriage, the husband comes alongside his wife and vice versa. Spousal togetherness desires oneness spiritually, emotionally, socially, and physically—all reflective of a God who wants to relate with his creation. Togetherness mandates the covenant focus. Husband and wife seek togetherness to be more like God, who made them image-bearers.

Yahweh dwelled with creation even when they sinned; he was there. So likewise, reconciliation means God comes near, seeking a reset in the relationship when one sins. He comes alongside and communicates his concerns. Consequences are neither ignored by God nor by one's spouse, but facing the blot on the relationship initiates a divine response to further alongside-ness.

Covenant Marriage is Sharing

Yahweh desires to share finitely with humanity. He shares his image in Creation with all men and women. Love as an action may not always be reciprocal since spurning love is possible. However, the bestowing of God's image enables the divine to share himself in a way that stamps finite elements of divinity on humanity. The sharing of his image conveys his care and ownership of his creation. Humanity is still made in God's image despite those who may renounce this imprint. Furthermore, the *male-and-female* image of God on humanity hints at the forthcoming unity in marriage. From Adam comes male and female, but they soon join together again in oneness by marriage. The unity of their Creation continues in their marital harmony, which consists of cleaving, becoming, and relating openly. The account radiates with uniting together, which culminates with marriage.

Much like intimacy, sharing can result in spurred love, but real intimacy needs a relationship and a shared betweenness from both sides. The space between the lover and the beloved is intimacy. Intimacy exists when two share knowledge, needs, desires, or personal aspects of each other. Covenant marriage shares, but the relationship can deepen or be shallow. However, the definition of covenant marriage expects pursuit and mutual self-sacrifice. The sharing in marriage imitates how our Creator shares himself with us by saving and dwelling with us.

A Covenant Ethos Pursues

Yahweh is not aloof—he actively pursues and interacts with Creation. Adam does not instigate the prompting for salvation; Yahweh himself does that. The replaced sacrifice of Abraham on the mount was not prompted by the patriarch but by God himself. Our God is a God who embarks on the uncomfortable and provides salvation. His covenant ethos encourages him to pursue his beloved. The husband and wife echo this prompting. Both instigate love and pursue the other, even when inconvenient. To prevent or ignore love is the opposite of the spirit of pursuing. A lover seeks the beloved, resembling the identity in a covenant bond.

The covenant identity in Ephesians 5 directs the husband and wife in sacrificial actions depicted in terms like submission, headship, and love. How does one reflect the covenant ethos in headship or submission in these household codes? The husband is indirectly tasked with headship in the wife's section, but the stress of covenantal love dominates in his section. His consecrated covenantal task toward his wife focuses his energies on loving her. Like God, he resembles a sacrificial lover who pursues, provides, and comes alongside his beloved. Likewise, the wife pursues also like a sacrificial lover yet with respect and submission toward the husband.

The wife's submission is not based on precisely defined placements in the relationship but on the covenant ethos of oneness and unity, which both desire to emulate. Neither task (headship or submission) attempts to pursue one's spouse in a pre-conditioned environment or placement. The husband does not wait for the wife to respect him before he loves, nor does the wife. She doesn't wait for her husband's love before she submits. Again, the mutual pursuit of unity in their relationship through these actions depicts the covenant tendency.

Covenant pursuit toward oneness prioritizes and simultaneously counters aloofness in the marriage. The focus of the marriage is reflecting their new identity in Christ, desiring Christ-likeness. The

110

aspects of submission and headship exist to guide specific areas for a semblance of order. Still, these areas never act like Contract Conformity, where set places promote substantial obligations, destroying intimacy and mutual pursuit.

Covenant Marriage is Sacrificial

God introduces a way to fulfill Adam's need in the first marriage when he created Eve, placing Adam as a sacrificial giver of his own flesh. The Creator starts reconciliation when Adam sins, and eventually, he provides the coverage of animal skins to cover the shame of sin. In God's story, the divine is the lover, and we are the beloved. Covenant marriage mimics the lover/beloved image when husband and wife pursue love, unity, and sacrificial tendencies. Both lover and beloved desire a greater oneness.

The sacrificial nature continues in salvation, where God provides and initiates sacrifice (the cross) for the beloved. Likewise, unexpected, initiated sacrifice characterizes the relationship in a covenant marriage. Biblical salvation is never just an issue of authority, rights, or obligations but provides a noble example of love. The sacrificial roles in marriage serve and relate one to another. Likewise, Christianity never heightens who is the leader or who has the authority but accentuates the identity to love, sacrifice and serve one another. Biblical marriage mirrors these qualities.

Sacrificial ideals in marriage never prioritize the individual's rights but the whole marital relationship, encouraging a precedent for one's

> Covenant marriage mimics the lover/beloved image when husband and wife pursue love, unity and sacrificial tendencies with each other.

spouse. The "us" of "you" and "me" is the focus, the center. Together, they mutually consider how they fulfill each other's needs. The covenant unity is greater than the individuals because a more excellent value is evident—reflecting Yahweh's covenant-making nature.

God's nature also shows up in his unconditional promises of eternal life for those who receive the Lord Jesus (John 1:12, 5:24). The believer lives more than a religious experience but a new identity as a child of God. The promise of eternal life guarantees this identity since

111

the Holy Spirit seals the believer (Eph. 1:13). A new identity asserts the lover and beloved motif in a covenant marriage. The unconditional manner of God's love provokes promises to underpin marriage. This covenant commitment of unconditional promises marks a critical difference between covenant and contract marriage. When the relationship breaks down, then reconciliation steps in. Again, much like Yahweh, His presence in the marriage motivates the couple to draw near and pursue a resolution lovingly, not forcefully.

Contract Marriage Reflects Islamic Conformity

Now, let's examine how some foundational concepts about Allah and Islam promote a contractual understanding of marriage. The basis of Islam depends on a Sunnah, the messenger's Path, and Guidance. The motivation to submit is often more external than internal, and the model is the life of the Islamic messenger. John Witte, Jr., a law professor at Emory University, observed, "The Muslim tradition rooted marriage not only in the teachings of the Qur'an but also in the example of Mohammed."[136] The Path of the messenger, especially the traditions, presents many examples of how he treated and responded to his wives to help Muslims answer questions concerning marital issues. So, Muslims affirm their prophet's example as the basis to conform to contract marriage. How he lived with his wives exemplifies the code for marriage. In this way, contract marriage reflects conformity to the Islamic Path.

As we know, Allah is alone and has no partners; neither can he share himself. Absolute Oneness does not allow another. The non-reflective manner of a contract marriage relies on the outcomes of an Absolute Oneness deity. Contract marriage absorbs the traits of Allah's work more than reflects his essence. Contract marriage cannot reflect Allah since he has no partner or association. Since absorption often depicts a one-way process, Islamic contract marriage travels a similar route. Islam never states that marriage reflects Allah, but one may conclude that the concept of marriage absorbs Islamic ideas. The goal of the Islamic marriage reflects more their messenger than any reflection of Allah.

112

Contract Marriage is Placement

Contract Marriage absorbs traits of an Absolute Oneness deity that prioritizes placement over a relationship, furthering the Creation status. The pre-determined place within Creation in which Adam's place over angels and all humanity's obligatory submission to Allah highlights humanity's position rather than a relationship with him.

Allah places the caliphate on earth with mandated Guidance. Humanity is to do and submit, a directive absorbed in the contract marriage. Together as mates, they walk the Path of Islam and maintain the religious honor expected. In al-Jibaly's book *The Quest for Love & Mercy*, he lists advantages for those married, which he calls "Preservation of Faith and Religion." He quotes a Hadith, which says, "When Allah grants one a righteous wife, He has helped him (by that) to preserve half of his religion. Let him then fear and revere Allah in regard to the other half."[137] In conjunction with this thought, he quotes another hadith, "Marriage is a *sunnah* (way) of mine, and whoever does not follow my *Sunnah* is not of my followers."[138] Marriage and following the proper *Sunnah* go hand in hand with the Islamic community expecting all Muslims to marry. When one marries, they observe a key directive of the *Sunnah*, placing them into the Muslim society and telling them how to act.

Contract marriage absorbs this thinking because the marriage powerfully protects the believing community. "Marriage completes half of one's faith . . . Completion of one's half of faith implies that mere marriage itself brings about many good qualities within a person, i.e., prevention from fornication and adultery, prevention from evil gazes."[139] In Islam, the thinking that marriage completes half their faith often refers to protection from sexual sins. The act of marriage empowers one to comply more with one's religion and to find the power to deal with sexual temptation. One book by Saiful Islam, *Marriage the Complete Solution,* alludes to the problem of singleness. For Muslims, marriage solves the problem of sexual desire and singleness.

The Islamic placement assumed that all would marry. Islamic contract marriage programs for power and protection to each Muslim community member. Much like Islamic Creation, the above statements see an adherent's position and place in Islam. In the assigned way, each person must submit to religious obligations that continue in the marriage relationship. The married couple follows the *Sunnah,* which defines their place as husband and wife.

Contract Marriage is Positional

Allah is above His creation; man is above angels; likewise, the husband enjoys a position above his wife. Placement defines the Islamic order, but positions correspond to responsibility to another. Submission to Allah's decrees, Will, and Guidance are essential to a proper, orderly way of living that parallels the positions within a marriage. This placement in the Islamic social order expects marital positions for the husband and wife.

As in any marriage, a relationship exists, but the priority of a contract marriage focuses on the husband's position as a ruler and the wife's position below to adhere to her husband's desires. The structure of rights and obligations is non-negotiable for the husband and wife. Their marriage functions on these Islamic ideas.

In considering the Absolute Oneness deity, al-Tamimi said, "It is impossible for two to share in the absolute *highest* description, because if both were equal from every angle, none [neither] of the two would be *higher* than the other. If on the other hand, they are not equal, the one depicted with *the highest* description would, therefore, only be one of them. Hence, it is impossible for the one who possesses the *highest* description to have a like or rival."[140] Repeating this quote here reveals how Islamic marriage absorbs this worldview since the two spouses are not considered equals together but occupy two orderly positions. This order, which dominates the ethos of contract marriage, attempts to eliminate rivalry within the union—the husband and wife as mates, which does not mean they are *like* each other but a match. To be like in oneness or equality would establish a basis for potential competition. The focus on position dominates the marital roles so that the structure of Islamic marriage avoids oneness and establishes a non-rival framework. The Islamic moral structure in the contract marriage forms an established social order.

Much like Absolute Oneness, the husband's position consumes the perspective—he has power and the right to be in that place. The husband and wife can live out the Will of the Absolute Oneness when

114

they submit to the set regulations. Their marriage union follows this common purpose of submission and continually seeks to maintain the ordained positions given.

Twoness of Contract Marriage

Contract Islamic marriage never forms oneness. Only Allah is one, and so this word *oneness* for Muslims customarily becomes reserved to describe only deity, never marriage. In contrast to covenant marriage's oneness, contract marriage forms a social agreement but never represents a metaphysical unity. Instead, contract marriage emphasizes twoness, in which separateness defines the connection more than unity. Twoness in marriage occurs when two persons exist independently with some connection. Yet, this separateness of obligations or rights represents the connection more than any form of oneness.

Placement and positioning in a contract marriage form more a twoness or duality than any semblance of oneness in marriage. Absolute Oneness cannot reflect, so a form of duality or twoness is evident. Twoness happens when the care for structure and individual rights dominates more than a concern for the marital mate's desires or needs. The pre-set positions of a husband and wife separate them into distinct roles, which require maintaining twoness. A widow from Tabriz, Iran, demonstrates the twoness concept when she says, *When you marry, in Iran, the relatives will say, "You have to have a separate bank account." From day one, you separate the bride's money. They show the husband's family as the enemy; they will be against you, so prepare your way to defend your way. They encourage a process of separation.*

Since I was never able to live in Iran, her words were profound to me. The backdrop of twoness-type thinking alludes to the husband's dominant role and the dowry or provisions for the wife. Only what he provides for her becomes her own, so this money allows her "to defend [her] way." Separateness starts at the wedding and continues throughout the contract marriage. Not all Islamic marriages are this way, but the structures and requirements espoused in the Islamic literature tend toward twoness, not oneness.

As mentioned, covenant marriage builds on the idea of sharing. Still, a contract marriage instead excludes mutuality for their relationship since each mate, especially the bride, will need to guard their funds and position and prepare to defend the little finances that one has. In this sense, contract marriage is neither oneness nor based on mutual sharing but a form of twoness that guards one's position, person, and assets.

Socially, since Islamic marriage allows polygamy, the wife's relationship with her husband is neither unique nor exclusive. Regardless of the state of polygamy in Islamic societies as normative, the husband's family can consist of multiple wives, up to four. Socially, this allowance illustrates a further separateness in the Islamic marriage idea, thus making the concept of marital oneness null and void. Oneness becomes impossible when a husband has two, three, or even four wives. In a covenant marriage, their exclusiveness protects their marriage unity. Oneness describes the Islamic idea concerning deity but undermines the ideals of Islamic marriage.

Contract Marriage Expects Service

Service centers any contract by expecting service and pursuing obligations. The Islamic Path is a way full of expectations and obligations. In contract marriage, the husband has rights over his wife, which Islamic marriage books consistently list. The *Ahadith* expanded the rights defined in the Quran. In *Marriage: A Complete Solution*, the author lists the husband's fifteen rights over his wife.[141] Contract marriage expects service, which often resembles the husband's privileges and the wife's obligations. Islamic literature clearly describes these multiple areas of service and duties, but for our purpose here, the key ideas guide our contrast. Islam expects submission, and contract marriage expects service. These ideas interlock and create a connection that Muslims do not ignore.

Conclusion

At their foundations, the Bible promotes covenant, the Quran contract. This exploration takes steps to go below the surface; underneath lies more than some ancient kiln or archaeological artifacts but constructed structures to define and categorize a contract or covenant model. These explored openings explain why each faith diverges when met in society, particularly with marriage. Islam's submission mandate thoroughly permeates every aspect of their faith and social relationships, especially marriage. Also, the Bible sincerely endorses a covenant perspective to influence every facet of belief and marriage.

When my son and I discovered the ancient kiln, we had no idea of the importance of this artifact to the local and national views. A few years after our adventure below the surface, the site became the main proof of historical evidence for the oldest site in the country, a point of great honor, especially for that region. Searching archaeological digs may not declare anything new under the sun, but the evidence benefits an attempt to understand what existed previously in that society. However, a new realization can grant a re-focus concerning perspectives, especially when the new understanding speaks to one's faith. Likewise, this search below biblical and quranic content gives a new view of why these circles differ.

I hope that *Searching Below the Surface* will give each of us new eyes to see the religious and marital landscapes, which differ in perspective because of their foundations. This search results in a new identity for believers from a contract background. They can see what formed their former community's landscape and now contrast the former by adopting a new identity to build a new perspective for their lives. For Muslims, their life and religion establish a contractual narrative, but the basis differs for the believer in Christ. The thoroughly covenantal description connects believers to Yahweh, who continually loves and pursues them as his beloved. Understanding these two distinct narratives will grant a better understanding of how to live today.

Case Study

Saeed and Ilham were distant cousins but married through an Islamic contract marriage. Their family felt this match would give them future security and hope. As relatives in the broader family network, they knew about each other but did not know each other socially. So first, their mothers, then their families came together. Ideas, hopes, and gifts were expectantly exchanged, and an engagement was initiated.

The wedding ceremony and preparations for this event connected the two sides of the family. Saeed and Ilham saw each other occasionally, but contact was limited until the marriage. Other families allowed engaged couples to get acquainted, but confinement was more the rule than contact. Their process included a negotiated dowry, partially received at the engagement and wedding. The families chose a key respected man on each side to negotiate and place any condition on the marriage.

Requesting the bride's consent took the standard time, with an honorable rejection promoted. Then, proper petitions and promises of affirmation for the bride from the groom were sent along to encourage the bride's acceptance. Eventually, she agreed, and the movement toward Arabic pronouncements to legally bind the marriage together took place. Both repeated the Arabic phrases to accept each other as husband and wife. Then the celebrations erupt since the two are now acceptable to each other as a married couple. The contract marriage is elaborate and defined. For Saeed and Ilham, the contract forms the basis of how they view marriage, which is tied to many rights and obligations. For them, the celebration only starts a lifetime of obligation together.

At their wedding, others did not know that Ilham sometimes had dreams about Jesus, and Saeed knew a believing Christian in his neighborhood. How will this Islamic contract marriage look when, in due time, the Spirit of God draws them to see the love of God in the Lord Jesus Christ? How will they define their marriage? Will they continue with contractual ideas or adapt covenant ones?

What do the Creation accounts impart for teachers who promote a contract or a covenant perspective? In considering roles, equality, and rights in marriage, what identity dominates for this couple? What does sexual intimacy look like for couples married contractually but now in Christ? And what biblical stories encourage oneness in marriage? In the explorations to follow, these questions will be answered.

To make personal comments, testimonies, and insights on this writing, please write me at

Nakhati.jon@gmail.com or #searchingbelow on Twitter @Nakhatij.

The NAKHATIJON.COM blog provides supplemental material on this subject.

For those interested in ministry to the least-reached, please get in touch with Christar.org

Appendix

Definition of Terms

Abrogation – The Islamic concept in which a later Quranic text replaces an earlier text. This process alters the former meaning or ruling to become an authorized cancellation procedure within Islam.

Absolute Oneness – A descriptive name of Allah who has no partners, son, or likeness, so he is utterly alone. The Arabic equivalent for Absolute Oneness is *Tawhid*.

Ahadith – Is the collection of transmitted hearsay statements of or about Mohammad. The most authentic collections are by al-Bukhara and Sahih Muslim, who compiled the sayings about 220 years after the death of Mohammad.

Allah – (الله) Is the Arabic name for God, used in the Quran.

Bismillah – An Arabic phrase that invokes Allah's name and mercy. Bismillah means "In the name of Allah."

Contract Conformity – Islamic compliance whereby each adherent seeks to abide by the proper socio-religious community (*Ummah*) obligations.

Contract Self-deliverance – Islamic Guidance grants humanity the capability to liberate themselves by following the stipulated dictates of Islam. The Islamic self-ability disallows any sense of lostness or need for a savior since each man or woman can submit to Islam for deliverance.

Divine Download – Translation of the Islamic word *wahy* (وحي) which means revelation. *Wahy* or revelation depicts a direct reveal from above, upon their messenger, without any participation of the messenger.

Guidance – The innate Allah-given human enablement to lead toward Islam.

Iblis – the Arabic name for Satan, who refused to bow to the Islamic Adam.

Indwelling Inspiration – The God-breathed process in which the Spirit of God generates through or intimately near the messenger the very words of God. The inspiration process mysteriously breathes through the personality of the messenger.

Indwelling Sanctification – The personal indwelling of the Spirit of God, which slowly transforms the believer toward Christlikeness. After a declaration of standing righteous in Christ, the believer's inward growth process starts with the indwelling presence of God to conform to his image (Rom. 8:29 and 2 Cor. 3:18) and fulfill the mandate *to love the Lord our God* (Deut. 6:5) with one's whole being.

Khalifa – The Arabic word describes the idea of vicegerent. A vicegerent establishes on the earth submission to Allah's rule.

Oneness in Unity (Trinity) – Describes the co-essence of divine persons within the Godhead that maintains oneness and harmony.

Partakers – Those who participate in God's creative works. In creation, humanity partakes of his divine image; in salvation, believers unite with Christ; and in sanctification, the Spirit of God indwells—all demonstrating a sharing of his divine actions. Believers are active participants in the many ways the God of the Bible shares himself, thus becoming partakers of the divine nature (2 Pet. 1:4).

Progressive Revelation – Describes God's act of incremental disclosure in revealing himself, his will, and his truth with new revelation, which always complements and supplements what has come before. The scriptures unfold to reveal more about God and espouse an ever-deepening knowledge concerning his plan. The sixty-six books of the Bible reveal God to be relational, close, and desirous to connect with humanity.

Revelation (Quran) – Islamic revelation precedes from above upon a detached messenger, promoting a purposeful disengagement to reveal Allah's will, not his person.

Revelation (Bible) – A self-revealing of God by various methods found in the Scriptures. In biblical inspiration, the Spirit breathes inward within or near an engaged messenger, moving him to write the very words of God. The one carried along by the Spirit forms a mystery alignment between God's Spirit and the messenger.

Sanctification – Covenant Sanctification involves a personal indwelling of God's Spirit so that a believer slowly transforms into Christ's likeness. In this new identity God grants, the believer dies to himself and gives way to the living Christ within, endeavoring to yield to the Spirit's direction.

—An inner relationship with God whereby each adherent seeks to abide by the internal leanings of the Holy Spirit, reflecting more of Christ each day.

Savior Salvation – Describes the deliverance which the Lord Jesus provided for any who will repent of their sins and believe that he is their Lord and Savior.

Shahada – The Muslim statement, "There is no God but Allah, and Muhammad is the messenger of Allah."

Shariat – The Islamic law encompasses the Quran, Sunnah, and the summary of jurisprudent consensus to promote Islamic social conformity for all Muslims. The *Shariat* guides the adherent to live a Muslim life.

Shirk – The sin of associating any partner with Allah's oneness.

Spectators – The distant onlookers of Allah's oneness in which Allah does not share himself nor indwell those who worship him. Muslims are only spectators of Allah's nature, never sharing or indwelt by the divine presence.

Sunnah – The primary source in Islamic law that establishes customs and beliefs summarizing the actions and sayings of their prophet, Muhammad, who becomes the model for adherents to follow Allah's will.

Sufis – A subset in either Sunni or Shia Islam that desires a direct, personal experience or union with Allah.

Surah – The Arabic name for quranic chapters.

Tawhid – Describes the absolute oneness of Allah's essence without partners.

Trinity – The unity of the divine persons: Father, Son, and Holy Spirit in oneness.

Twoness – A relationship where each mate exists independently of the other, yet some connection exists. A separateness defines the relational connection more than any unity. Twoness in marriage occurs when two people live independently in finances, decisions, and marital positions.

Ummah – Portrays the Islamic community that follows Allah's Guidance.

Unity – Depicts a joining of persons into an interrelation bond.

Vicegerent – Allah's bestowment of divine Guidance to humanity to rule over creation, including angels. This ruling as Allah's deputy includes an endowed with authority to enforce submission to Allah.

Aasi, Ghulam Haider. *Muslim Understanding*, n.d. or publisher.

Abdulati, Hammudah. *Islam in Focus*. Beltsville, MD: Amana, 1998.

Ali, Maulana Muhammad. *The Holy Qur'an with English Translation and Commentary*. Ohio: Ahmadiyya Anjuman Isha'at Islam Lahore, 2017.

Arkoun, Mohammed. *The Unthought in Contemporary Islamic Thought*, London: Saqi Books, 2002.

Asad, Muhammad. *Islam and Politics*. Al-Islam publications, n.d.

Badawi, Jamal. *Bridgebuilding between Christian and Muslim*. Halifax, NS: Islamic Information Foundation, n.d.

al-Badr, Abdur-Razzaq ibn Abdul-Muhsin. *The Book of Dhikr and Supplication in Accordance to the Quran and the Sunnah*. Translated by Waleed Bleyhesh al-Amri. Madinah: King Fahd Quran Printing Complex, 2004.

Bennett, Clinton. *Muslims and Modernity: Current Debates*. London: Continuum, 2005.

Bock, Darrell L., and Mikel Del Rosario. The Table Briefing: on the Heart of Islam. Interview with Imad Shehadeh. *Bibliotheca Sacra* 171 (2014).

Calhoun, Susanne. "The Spirit's Indwelling," in *Lexham Survey of Theology*, ed. Mark Ward et al. (Bellingham, WA: Lexham Press, 2018).

Chambers, Oswald. *My Utmost for His Highest: Selections for the Year* (Grand Rapids, MI: Oswald Chambers Publications; Marshall Pickering, 1986.

Deere, Jack S. "Deuteronomy," in *The Bible Knowledge Commentary: An Exposition of the Scriptures*, ed. J. F. Walvoord and R. B. Zuck, vol. 1 (Wheaton, IL: Victor Books, 1985).

Doornbos, Gayle. "God's Unity," in *Lexham Survey of Theology*, ed. Mark Ward et al. Bellingham, WA: Lexham Press, 2018.

Duderija, Adis. *The Sunna and its Status in Islamic Law*. New York: Palgrave MacMillan, 2016.

Erickson, Millard J. *Christian Theology*, 3rd ed. Grand Rapids, MI: Baker Academic, 2013.

al-Faruqi, Isma'il R. *Islam*, Beltsville, MD: Amana Publications, 1998.

Al Fiqh al Akbar: An Accurate Translation. SunnahMuakada.com, 2014, pdf.

Frame, John. "The Bible's Inspiration," in *Lexham Survey of Theology*, ed. Mark Ward et al. (Bellingham, WA: Lexham Press, 2018.

Gangel, Kenneth O. *Acts*, vol. 5, Holman New Testament Commentary. Nashville, TN: Broadman & Holman Publishers, 1998.

Gatje, Helmut. *The Qur'an and its Exegesis: Selected Texts with Classical and Modern Muslim Interpretations*, ed and tr. Alford T Welch, Oxford: One World, 1997.

al-Ghazali. *Kitab Sharh Aja'ib al-Qalb*. Translated by R. J. McCarthy in *Deliverance from Error*. Louisville: Twayne Publishers, 1980.

Gilchrist, John. *The Qur'an: The Scripture of Islam*. South Africa: Life Challenge Africa, 2003.

Goffman, Erving. *The Presentation of Self in Everyday Life*. London: Penguin, 1990.

Haleem, Muhammad Abdel. "Quranic Arabic" Indexed in Seyyed Hossein Nasr, Caner K. Dagli, Maria Massi Dakake, Joseph E. B. Lumbard. *The Study Quran*. New York: HarperCollins, 2015.

Hamidullah, Mohammad. *The Emergence of Islam*. Translated and edited by Afzal Iqbal. New Delhi: Adam Publishers, 2010.

Hanifa, Imam Abu. Translated by Abdur Rahman ibn Yusuf. *Al Fiqh al Akbar: An Accurate Translation*. sunnahMuakada.com, pdf.

Harris, W. Hall, III, Elliot Ritzema, Rick Brannan, Douglas Mangum, John Dunham, Jeffrey A. Reimer, and Micah Wierenga, eds. *The Lexham English Bible*. Bellingham, WA: Lexham Press, 2012.

Heiser, Michael S. "Image of God," ed. John D. Barry et al., *The Lexham Bible Dictionary*. Bellingham, WA: Lexham Press, 2016.

Huey, F. B. *Jeremiah, Lamentations*, vol. 16, The New American Commentary. Nashville: Broadman & Holman Publishers, 1993.

Hussain, Amjad M. *The Muslim Creed: A Contemporary Theological Study*. Cambridge: The Islamic Texts Society, 2016.

Hye, Abdul. *What Every Woman Should Know*. Houston: Where do you stand publishers, 2002.

Idris, Jaafar Sheikh. "Is Man the Vicegerent of God?" *Journal of Islamic Studies*, Vol. 1 (1990). www.jstor.org/stable/26195669.

Islam, Saiful. *Marriage: A Complete Solution*. West Yorkshire: JKN Publications, 2011.

al-Jibaly, Muhammad Mustafa. *The Quest for Love & Mercy*. Arlington: al-Kitaab & as-Sunnah Publishing, 2005.

Jon, Nakhati. *Teaching Marriage from Genesis.* Unpublished material, 2020.

Jon, Nakhati. *Survey of Shia Marriage in Iran.* Amazon, 2018.

al-Karim, Muhammad 'Abd. *Kitab Niyayah al-Aqdam fi'Ilm al-Kalam, (Maktabah al-Thaqafah al-Diniyyah).* 2nd Ed. Bayrut: Dar al-Kutub al-'Ilmiyyah, 2nd Ed., 1992.

Lange, John Peter, et al., *A Commentary on the Holy Scriptures: Genesis.* Bellingham, WA: Logos Bible Software, 2008.

Lea, Thomas D., and Hayne P. Griffin, *1, 2 Timothy, Titus*, vol. 34, The New American Commentary. Nashville: Broadman & Holman Publishers, 1992.

Litwak, Kenneth D. "Sanctification," ed. Douglas Mangum et al., *Lexham Theological Wordbook.* Lexham Bible Reference Series. Bellingham, WA: Lexham Press, 2014.

Manser, Martin H. *Dictionary of Bible Themes: The Accessible and Comprehensive Tool for Topical Studies.* London: Martin Manser, 2009.

Marar, Ziyad. *Intimacy*, Routledge, 2014, EBSCO.

Mathews, K. A. *Genesis 1–11:26*, vol. 1A, The New American Commentary. Nashville: Broadman & Holman Publishers, 1996.

Maududi, Sayyid Abul A'la. *Ethical Viewpoint of Islam.* Lahore: Islamic Publications, 5th edition, 1979.

Memaryan, Nadereh et al. "Spirituality Concept by Health Professionals in Iran: A Qualitative Study" *Evidence-Based Complementary and Alternative Medicine.* Volume 2016, Article ID 8913870. www.hindawi.com

Mir, Mustansir. *Religion & Literature*, vol 20:1 "The Literature of Islam" Spring, 1988.

al-Mo'taz, Abdullah bin Muhammad. *The Man: A Strange Creature with Diverse Qualities.* Houston: Darussalam, 1997.

Nasr, Seyyed Hossein, Caner K. Dagli, Maria Massi Dakake, Joseph E. B. Lumbard. *The Study Quran.* New York: HarperCollins, 2015.

Nasr, Seyyed Hossein. *Ideals and Realities of Islam.* London: George Allen & Unwin, 1975.

Nooruddin, 'Allaman. Trans. Amatul Rahman 'Omar and 'Abdul Mannan 'Omar. *The Holy Qur'an Hockessin*, DE: Noor Foundation, 2016.

Palmer, Paul F. "Christian Marriage: Contract or Covenant?" *Theological Studies*, 33, no. 4 (1972): 619. ATLA Serials.

Philips, Abu Ameenah Bilal. *The Fundamentals of Tawhid (Islamic Monotheism)*. 2nd edition. Riyadh: International Islamic Publishing House, 2005.

Philips, A. B. *Did God Become Man?* 1495 Hijri (2018), eBook on www.islamreligion.com.

Pickthall, Muhammad M. ed., *The Quran*. Medford, MA: Perseus Digital Library, n.d.

Qureshi, Nabeel. *Seeking Allah, Finding Jesus*. Grand Rapids: Zondervan, 2018, e-book.

Schaff, Philip. *History of the Christian Church*. 5th ed. Grand Rapids: Eerdmans, 1981.

------ *The Ante-Nicene Fathers* Grand Rapids, MI: Wm. B. Eerdmans, 1976.

Saeed, Abdullah. "Rethinking 'Revelation' as a Precondition for Reinterpreting the Qur'an: a Qur'anic Perspective." *Journal of Islamic Studies*. Edinburgh: University Press, Vol 1:1, 1999. www.jstor.org/stable/25727946

Salleh, Mohd Fuad Mohd. *Introduction to Islam: Islam the System of Life*. Universiti Selangor, 2015, pdf.

Sanders, Fred. "The Doctrine of Scripture and Revelation," in *Lexham Survey of Theology*, ed. Mark Ward et al. Bellingham, WA: Lexham Press, 2018.

Shakir, M. H. ed., *The Quran*. Medford, MA: Perseus Digital Library, n.d.

Shehadeh, Imad N. *God with Us and without Us*. Cumbria: Langham Publishing, 2018.

Shehadi, Fadlou. *Ghazali's Unique Unknowable God*. Leiden: E.J. Brill, 1964.

Siddiqi, Muzammil H. "Salvation in Islamic Perspective" *Islamic Studies* Vol 32:1, 1993.

Sproul, R. C. *Can I Trust the Bible?* vol. 2, The Crucial Questions Series. Lake Mary, FL: Reformation Trust Publishing, 2009.

Steppat, Fritz. "God's Deputy: Materials on Islam's Image of Man" *Arabica* Vol: 36:2, July 1989, 163–172.

al-Tamimi, Muhammad ibn Khalifah. *Tawhid of Allah's Most Beautiful Names & Lofty Attributes*. Abu Safwan Farid Haibatan, translator. Birmingham: Al-Hidaayah Publishing, 2002.

Tozer, A.W. *The Knowledge of the Holy*. New York: Harper & Row, 1975.

'Ulwan, 'Abdullah Nasih. *Islam and Sex*. Trans. Khalifa Ezzat, Cairo: Dar al-Salam, 2011.

Yancey, Philip. *What's So Amazing About Grace?* Grand Rapids, Michigan: Zondervan Publishing House, 1997.

Yusuf Ali, Abdullah. *The Holy Qur'an*. Brentwood, Maryland: Amana, 1983.

Wickwire, Dan. *Has the Bible Been Changed?* Aneko Press, self-published e-book, 2014.

Wiersbe, Warren W. *The Bible Exposition Commentary*, vol. 2. Wheaton, IL: Victor Books, 1996.

Witte, Jr. John. "More than a Mere Contract: Marriage as Contract and Covenant in Law and Theology." *Religion and Culture Web Forum*, May 2008.

Zakiyyah, Umm. *Let's Talk About Sex and Muslim Love: Essays on Intimacy and Romantic Relationships in Islam—Maryland*: Al-Walaa, eBook, 2016.

Internet Resources

1. aboutislam.net/counseling/ask-about-islam/is-guidance-a-divine-gift/ accessed Sept. 30, 2021.

2. Al-Hilali, Muhammad Taqi-ud-Din and Muhammad Muhsin Khan. *The Noble Quran*. www.iium.edu.my/deed/quran/nobelquran_arabic/index.html

3. Al-Huzhriyyah, Abdah. //aljumuah.com/the-ultimate-book-what-is-the-quran-and-how-did-it-come-to-prophet-muhammad/

4. Ali, Shaykh Ahmad. www.youtube.com/watch?v=2CB0aCYoa6U

5. www.al-islam.org/philosophy-islamic-laws-nasir-makarim-shirazi-jafar-subhani/question-98-man-superior-angels

6. www.biblegateway.com/versions/English-Standard-Version-ESV-Bible/

7. www.biblegateway.com/versions/JB-Phillips-New-Testament/

8. www.christianpost.com/news/fastest-growing-church-has-no-buildings-no-central-leadership-and-is-mostly-led-by-women.html

9. en.wikipedia.org/wiki/Iblis

10. www.graceguy.org/blog-posts/whats-so-unique-about-christianity-cs-lewis-answers

11. www.islamicinsights.com/religion/forgetfulness.html

12. islamqa.info/en/answers/50774/he-is-debating-with-a-christian-and-is-asking-does-god-have-a-spirit

13. www.islamreligion.com/articles/10033/islamic-concept-of-spirituality/

14. www.islamreligion.com/articles/11340/guidance-in-islam/

15. islamtomorrow.com/true_religion.asp

16. Orchard, Bashir Ahmad. *Eye Uplifted* www.reviewofreligions.org/5939/the-concept-of-islamic-society/

17. *The Oxford Dictionary of Islam.* Edited by John L. Esposito. *Oxford Islamic Studies Online,* www.oxfordislamicstudies.com/article/opr/t125/e666

18. www.oxfordislamicstudies.com/article/opr/t243/e332

19. www.oxfordislamicstudies.com/article/opr/t125/e758

20. *Pasha, Sayed Hameedullah Nusrat.* www.reviewofreligions.org/5582/absolute-oneness/

21. Rudd, Steve. www.bible.ca/trinity/trinity-oneness-unity-yachid-vs-echad

22. www.tandfonline.com/doi/pdf/10.1179/175355210X1274781848 321 accessed April 3, 2020. This is an excellent summary of how archeology is manipulated for political purposes.

23. Walton, John. www.youtube.com/watch?v=AnPQgby8oKI

24. www.wonderopolis.org/wonder/how-do-mirrors-work

25. understandquran.com/know-allah/

26. www.youtube.com/watch?v=EfpAPQLUrM4 "Adam" accessed March 29, 2020.

Topic Index

---

[1] All quotes are from ESV (English Standard Version) unless noted otherwise.

[2] I will use *Oneness in Unity* or Trinity of Oneness as a proper noun to describe Trinity. Likewise, *Absolute Oneness* will be the appropiate noun for the Islamic belief.

[3] M. H. Shakir, ed., *The Quran* (Medford, MA: Perseus Digital Library, n.d.).

[4] احد

[5] *Sayed Hameedullah Nusrat Pasha.* www.reviewofreligions.org/5582/absolute-oneness/ accessed March 23, 2019.

[6] M. H. Shakir, ed., *The Quran* (Medford, MA: Perseus Digital Library, n.d.).

[7] An Arabic phrase that invokes Allah's name and mercy. Bismillah says, "In the name of Allah."

[8] Muslims see the idea of the "Son of God" in a physical sense yet believe in His virgin birth. Apologetically, stressing the spiritual understanding of his sonship becomes more relevant since he was miraculously born of a virgin (Luke 1:34,35), which even Muslims believe.

[9] This Islamic sect strives to formulate strong apologetic responses to non-Muslims. Many Muslims consider them to be "non-Muslims." I mentioned their material since their writings dominate the English world.

[10] *Sayed Hameedullah Nusrat Pasha.* www.reviewofreligions.org/5582/absolute-oneness/ accessed March 23, 2019.

[11] Muhammad ibn Khalifah al-Tamimi. *Tawhid of Allah's Most Beautiful Names & Lofty Attributes.* Abu Safwan Farid Haibatan, translator. Birmingham: Al-Hidaayah Publishing, 2002, 117. Al-Tamimi is an Islamic Professor at al-Madinah University in Saudi Arabia.

[12] Imad N. Shehadeh. *God With Us and Without Us*. (Cumbria: Langham Publishing, 2018), 81.

[13] A.W. Tozer. *The Knowledge of the Holy*. New York: Harper & Row, 1975, 23.

[14] When the text capitalizes LORD, this represents the Hebrew word, Yahweh.

[15] Muhammad M. Pickthall, ed., *The Quran* (Medford, MA: Perseus Digital Library, n.d.).

[16] Ibid.

[17] Tajik: *сегона,* Uzbek: *uchlik.*

[18] تثليث

[19] Al-Ghazali *Kitab Sharh Aja'ib al-Qalb*. Translated by R. J. McCarthy in *Deliverance from Error*. Louisville: Twayne Publishers, 1980, 190.

[20] C. S. Lewis, *Mere Christianity* (New York: HarperCollins, 1952), 175

[21] islamqa.info/en/answers/50774/he-is-debating-with-a-christian-and-is-asking-does-god-have-a-spirit accessed Jan. 18, 2020.

[22] Badawi, Jamal. *Bridgebuilding between Christian and Muslim* (Halifax, NS: Islamic Information Foundation, n.d.) 4.

[23] Amjad M. Hussain. *The Muslim Creed: A Contemporary Theological Study*, Cambridge: The Islamic Texts Society, 2016, 45.

[24] Modalism came from Sabellious, a third-century priest. A form of modalism is evidenced today in the movements known as "Jesus Only" or "Oneness Pentecostalism." These false teachings state the godhead as one but in different modes or manifestations as Father, Son and Spirit at different times. Neither Christianity nor Islam would accept this view of God.

[25] John Frame, "The Bible's Inspiration," in *Lexham Survey of Theology*, ed. Mark Ward et al. (Bellingham, WA: Lexham Press, 2018).

[26] Dan Wickwire. *Has the Bible Been Changed?* Aneko Press, self-published e-book, 2014, location 522. The last sentence is credited to Lewis Sperry Chafer.

[27] Warren W. Wiersbe, *The Bible Exposition Commentary*, vol. 2 (Wheaton, IL: Victor Books, 1996), 252.

[28] R. C. Sproul, *Can I Trust the Bible?* vol. 2, The Crucial Questions Series (Lake Mary, FL: Reformation Trust Publishing, 2009), 15–16.

[29] Ibid., 17.

[30] Mohammad Hamidullah. *The Emergence of Islam*. Translated and edited by Afzal Iqbal. New Delhi: Adam Publishers, 2010, 158-9.

[31] Leon Morris, *The Gospel according to Matthew*, The Pillar New Testament Commentary (Grand Rapids, MI; Leicester, England: W.B. Eerdmans; Inter-Varsity Press, 1992), 110.

[32] Imad Shehadeh. *God with us and without us*. Cumbria: Langham Partnership, 2018, 33.

[33] Ibid., 19.

[34] Abdullah Saeed. *Journal of Qur'anic Studies*. "Rethinking 'Revelation' as a Precondition for Reinterpreting the Qur'an: A Qur'anic Perspective" Edinburgh University Press, Vol 1:1, 1999, 108.

[35] Islam repeatedly categorizes "guidance" (هداية) as the means to know Islamic submission.

[36] Fred Sanders, "The Doctrine of Scripture and Revelation," in *Lexham Survey of Theology*, ed. Mark Ward et al. (Bellingham, WA: Lexham Press, 2018).

[37] وحي

[38] تنزيل "to send down" sometimes spelled *tanzeel*. Also, *nuzul*, "to come down."

[39] Pickthall's and Shakir's Quran.

[40] Nasr's *The Study Quran* and A. Yusuf Ali's *The Holy Qur'an*.

[41] Seyyed Hossein Nasr, Caner K. Dagli, Maria Massi Dakake, Joseph E. B. Lumbard. *The Study Quran*. New York: HarperCollins, 2015, 1607, "The Islamic View of the Quran" by Muhammad Mustafa al-Azami.

[42] Imam Abu Hanifa. Translated by Abdur Rahman Ibn Yusuf. *Al Fiqh al Akbar: An Accurate Translation*. sunnahMuakada.com, pdf, 35.

[43] Seyyed Hossein Nasr, Caner K. Dagli, Maria Massi Dakake, Joseph E. B. Lumbard. *The Study Quran*. New York: HarperCollins, 2015, note on Surah 42:51, 1187.

[44] Abdah Al-Huzhriyyah. aljumuah.com/the-ultimate-book-what-is-the-quran-and-how-did-it-come-to-prophet-muhammad/ accessed March 29, 2019. This website also gives many examples from the Hadiths supporting of their belief in the Quran coming down.

[45] Seyyed Hossein Nasr, Caner K. Dagli, Maria Massi Dakake, Joseph E. B. Lumbard. *The Study Quran*. New York: HarperCollins, 2015, 1626, "Quranic Arabic" by Muhammad Abdel Haleem.

[46] Ibid.

[47] However, A. Yusuf Ali's *The Holy Qur'an* uses the word, inspiration quite freely in the text (Surah 6:19) and his notes. I understand the reason for this is because he writes apologetically to the English world, especially since he adopted this word more than Islamic scholars normally would.

[48] Abdah Al-Huzhriyyah. aljumuah.com/the-ultimate-book-what-is-the-quran-and-how-did-it-come-to-prophet-muhammad/ accessed March 29, 2019.

[49] Maulana Muhammad Ali. *The Holy Qur'an with English Translation and Commentary*. Ohio: Ahmadiyya Anjuman Isha'at Islam Lahore, 2017, note on Surah 42:52, 952.

[50] Seyyed Hossein Nasr, Caner K. Dagli, Maria Massi Dakake, Joseph E. B. Lumbard. *The Study Quran*. New York: HarperCollins, 2015, note on Surah 42:52-3, 1187.

[51] Ibid.

[52] John C. Whitcomb, Jr. "Contemporary Apologetics and the Christian Faith" *Bibliotheca Sacra* July-September 1977, 198.

[53] Abdullah Saeed. *Journal of Qur'anic Studies*. "Rethinking 'Revelation' as a Precondition for Reinterpreting the Qur'an: A Qur'anic Perspective" Edinburgh University Press, Vol 1:1, 1999, 93. This quote posted online at: www.jstor.org/stable/25727946?seq=1 accessed March 19, 2020.

[54] Ghulam Haider Aasi. *Muslim Understanding*, n.d., 1.

[55] Mohammed Arkoun. *The Unthought in Contemporary Islamic Thought*, London: Saqi Books, 2002, 71.

[56] www.christianlingua.com

[57] C. S. Lewis *The Weight of Glory*,

[58] Mark 12:13–17, paraphrased.

[59] Millard J. Erickson, *Christian Theology*, 3rd ed. (Grand Rapids, MI: Baker Academic, 2013), 465.

[60] K. A. Mathews, *Genesis 1-11:26*, vol. 1A, The New American Commentary (Nashville: Broadman & Holman Publishers, 1996), 131.

[61] John Peter Lange et al., *A Commentary on the Holy Scriptures: Genesis* (Bellingham, WA: Logos Bible Software, 2008), 164.

[62] Muhammad ibn Khalifah al-Tamimi. *Tawhid of Allah's Most Beautiful Names & Lofty Attributes*. Abu Safwan Farid Haibatan, translator. Birmingham: Al-Hidaayah Publishing, 2002, 142.

[63] Ibid., 100.

[64] islamtomorrow.com/true_religion.asp accessed April 24, 2019.

[65] Harris, W. Hall, III, Elliot Ritzema, Rick Brannan, Douglas Mangum, John Dunham, Jeffrey A.

Reimer, and Micah Wierenga, eds. *The Lexham English Bible*. Bellingham, WA: Lexham Press, 2012, Genesis 2:7

[66] Specifics of the Genesis account are in *Explorations in Genesis*.

[67] Abu Ameenah Bilal Philips, *The Fundamentals of Tawhid (Islamic Monotheism)*. 2nd edition. Riyadh: International Islamic Publishing House, 2005, 28.

[68] Also see Al-Ghazali *Kitab Sharh Aja'ib al-Qalb*. Translated by R. J. McCarthy in *Deliverance from Error*. Louisville: Twayne Publishers, 1980, 310.

[69] Fadlou Shehadi. *Ghazali's Unique Unknowable God*. Leiden: E.J. Brill, 1964, 17.

[70] Ibid., 18.

[71] See Surah 15:29, 32:9, 38:72 and 66:12.

[72] Muhammad Taqi-ud-Din Al-Hilali and Muhammad Muhsin Khan. *The Noble Quran*. www.iium.edu.my/deed/quran/nobelquran_arabic/index.html accessed April 24, 2019. Al-Razi, a 12th century Persian Sunni theologian, proposed this view.

[73] Michael S. Heiser, "Image of God," ed. John D. Barry et al., *The Lexham Bible Dictionary* (Bellingham, WA: Lexham Press, 2016).

[74] Millard J. Erickson, *Christian Theology*, 3rd ed. (Grand Rapids, MI: Baker Academic, 2013), 470.

[75] Michael S. Heiser, "Image of God," ed. John D. Barry et al., *The Lexham Bible Dictionary* (Bellingham, WA: Lexham Press, 2016).

[76] Millard J. Erickson, *Christian Theology*, 3rd ed. (Grand Rapids, MI: Baker Academic, 2013), 464–465.

[77] Fadlou Shehadi. *Ghazali's Unique Unknowable God*. Leiden: E.J. Brill, 1964, 22.

[78] Sometimes called vicegerent. Some Muslim scholars only use the Arabic word, *Khalifa*.

[79] Successor seems older in use as current literature tends to use vicegerent or deputy. See Fritz Steppat "God's Deputy: Materials on Islam's Image of Man" *Arabica* Vol: 36:2, July 1989, 163–172.

[80] See Jaafar Sheikh Idris "Is Man the vicegerent of God?" *Journal of Islamic Studies*, Vol. 1 (1990), 100. www.jstor.org/stable/26195669 accessed Nov 18, 2019.

[81] www.youtube.com/watch?v=EfpAPQLUrM4 accessed March 29, 2020.

[82] Muhammad M. Pickthall, ed., *The Quran* (Medford, MA: Perseus Digital Library, n.d.).

[83] Hammudah Abdulati. *Islam in Focus*. Maryland: Amana, 1998, 52.

[84] Seyyed Hossein Nasr, Caner K. Dagli, Maria Massi Dakake, Joseph E. B. Lumbard. *The Study Quran*. New York: HarperCollins, 2015, Note on Surah 7:19

[85] www.al-islam.org/philosophy-islamic-laws-nasir-makarim-shirazi-jafar-subhani/question-98-man-superior-angels accessed Nov. 17, 2019.

[86] Surah 2:34, 7:11, 15:31-32, 17:61, 18:50, 20:116, 26:95, 34:20, 38:74-75.

[87] M. H. Shakir, ed., *The Quran* (Medford, MA: Perseus Digital Library, n.d.).

[88] Ibid.

[89] Hammudah Abdulati. *Islam in Focus*. Maryland: Amana, 1998, 52.

[90] M. H. Shakir, ed., *The Quran* (Medford, MA: Perseus Digital Library, n.d.).

[91] Message at Wheaton College 9/25/13. www.youtube.com/watch?v=AnPQgby8oKI accessed Nov. 30, 2019.

[92] Nabeel Qureshi. *Seeking Allah, Finding Jesus* (Grand Rapids: Zondervan, 2018), e-book, 201.

[93] www.hurriyetdailynews.com/culverts-scanned-in-3d-in-hagia-sophia-157035 accessed Aug. 1, 2020.

94 Ismail al-Faruqi, *Islam* (Niles, Illinois: Argus Communications, 1979), 9.

95 The Muslim statement, "There is no God but Allah, and Muhammad is the messenger of Allah."

96 فطرة

97 aboutislam.net/counseling/ask-about-islam/is-guidance-a-divine-gift/ This blog connects these ideas. Accessed Sept. 30, 2021.

98 "The Road Not Taken" Published 1915, now in the public domain.

99 A. B. Philips. *Did God Become Man?* 1495 Hijri (2018), 14. eBook on www.islamreligion.com accessed Nov. 14, 2019.

100 www.whyislam.org/on-faith/festival-of-the-sacrifice/ accessed Sept. 10, 2020.

101 M. H. Shakir, ed., *The Quran* (Medford, MA: Perseus Digital Library, n.d.).

102 www.islamreligion.com/articles/11340/guidance-in-islam/ accessed Nov 14, 2019.

103 A Shia who leads in remembering the martyrdom of Hussein. This man previously chanted the Islamic verses publicly for this occasion.

104 Rom. 8:26–29, John 17:17; Acts 20:32.

105 1 Cor 15:41–58; Rom. 8:18–25; Rev. 21.

106 "The Road Not Taken" Published 1915, Public domain.

107 Paul F. Palmer. "Christian Marriage: Contract or Covenant?" *Theological Studies*, 33, no. 4 (1972): 619. ATLA Serials.

108 Way of the prophet.

109 Abdur-Razzaq ibn Abdul-Muhsin al-Badr. *The Book of Dhikr and Supplication in Accordance to the Quran and the Sunnah.* Translated by Waleed Bleyhesh al-Amri. Madinah: King Fahd Quran Printing Complex, 2004, 7.

110 W. Hall Harris III et al., eds, *The Lexham English Bible* (Bellingham, WA: Lexham Press, 2012), Jer. 31:33–34.

111 F. B. Huey, *Jeremiah, Lamentations*, vol. 16, The New American Commentary (Nashville: Broadman & Holman Publishers, 1993), 284.

112 www.youtube.com/watch?v=2CB0aCYoa6U accessed Nov. 15, 2019. By Shaykh Ahmad Ali.

113 In the video, his chair *arsh*, and throne *kursi* are prominent.

114 understandquran.com/know-allah/ accessed Nov. 15, 2019.

115 A. B. Philips. *Did God Become Man?* 1495 Hijri (2018), 25. E-book on www.islamreligion.com accessed Nov. 14, 2019.

116 At this point, Contract Conformity as a proper noun will define the specific form of Islamic "sanctification."

117 Susanne Calhoun, "The Spirit's Indwelling," in *Lexham Survey of Theology*, ed. Mark Ward et al. (Bellingham, WA: Lexham Press, 2018). Italics mine.

118 Oswald Chambers, *My Utmost for His Highest: Selections for the Year* (Grand Rapids, MI: Oswald Chambers Publications; Marshall Pickering, 1986).

119 Abdullah bin Muhammad al-Mo'taz. *The Man: A Strange Creature with Diverse Qualities.* Houston: Darussalam, 1997, 54.

120 Umm Zakiyyah. *Let's Talk About Sex and Muslim Love: Essays on Intimacy and Romantic Relationships in Islam.* Maryland: Al-Walaa, eBook, 2016, 24.

121 Muhammad Asad. *Islam and Politics.* Al-Islam publications, n.d.

122 Sayyid Abul a'la Maududi. *Ethical Viewpoint of Islam.* Trans. By Khurshid Ahmad. (Lahore: Islamic Publications, 1979), 24.

123 www.oxfordislamicstudies.com/article/opr/t243/e332 accessed Nov. 23, 2019.

124 These areas are mentioned by Abdullah bin Muhammad al-Mo'taz. *The Man: A Strange Creature with Diverse Qualities.* Houston: Darussalam, 1997, 13.

[125] www.oxfordislamicstudies.com/article/opr/t125/e758 accessed Nov. 23, 2019.

[126] Sahih al-Bukhari collected by 846 AD and Sahih Muslim collected by 870 AD.

[127] Adis Duderija. *The Sunna and its Status in Islamic Law*. (New York: Palgrave MacMillan, 2016), 5. Recited is *wahi matlu*, while unrecited is *wahi ghayr matlu*. See *Muslims and Modernity: Current Debates* by Clinton Bennett, 87.

[128] www.iium.edu.my/deed/lawbase/al_majalle/al_majalleb15.html accessed Nov 3, 2021.

[129] Abdul Hye. *What every Woman should Know*. Houston: Where do you stand publishers, 2002, 89.

[130] A. Yusuf Ali. *The Holy Qur'an*. (Brentwood, Md: Amana, 1983), Note on Surah 24:54, #3030, 914.

[131] A. Yusuf Ali. *The Holy Qur'an*. (Brentwood, Md: Amana, 1983), surah 3:85, note 418, 145.

[132] 33-yr-old male, 2020

[133] Ghulam Haider Aasi, *Muslim Understanding*, n.d., 38.

[134] Surah 1:6. This statistic is found in Bahsir Ahmad Orchard's *Eye Uplifted* on www.reviewofreligions.org/5939/the-concept-of-islamic-society/ accessed Jan 18, 2020.

[135] مثنوى معنوى

[136] John Witte, Jr. "More than a Mere Contract: Marriage as Contract and Covenant in Law and Theology." *Religion and Culture Web Forum*, May 2008, 13.

[137] Muhammad Mustafa al-Jibaly. *The Quest for Love & Mercy*. (Arlington: Al-Kitaab & as-Sunnah Publishing, 2005), 10.

[138] Ibid. 7.

[139] Islam, *Marriage a Complete Solution*, 14

[140] Muhammad ibn Khalifah al-Tamimi. *Tawhid of Allah's Most Beautiful Names & Lofty Attributes*. Abu Safwan Farid Haibatan, translator. (Birmingham: Al-Hidaayah Publishing, 2002), 117. Italic is mine.

[141] Saiful Islam. *Marriage: A Complete Solution*. West Yorkshire: JKN Publications, 2011, 73.

www.ingramcontent.com/pod-product-compliance
Lightning Source LLC
Chambersburg PA
CBHW061731020426
42331CB00006B/1194